WEALTH
PROTECTION
PLANNING

For Orthopaedic Surgeons and Sports Medicine Specialists

Four Quick Lessons on Asset Protection, Tax Reduction and Developing a Thriving Practice in Sports Medicine

Second Edition

Peter J. Millett MD, MSc
David B. Mandell, JD, MBA
Jason M. O'Dell, MS, CWM
Carole C. Foos, CPA

with contributing author
Cheyenne Brinson, CPA, MBA
of Karen Zupko and Associates

Guardian
Publishing LLC

2017

WEALTH PROTECTION PLANNING FOR ORTHOPAEDIC SURGEONS AND SPORTS MEDICINE SPECIALISTS: FOUR QUICK LESSONS ON ASSET PROTECTION, TAX REDUCTION AND DEVELOPING A THRIVING PRACTICE IN SPORTS MEDICINE

By Peter J. Millett, MD, MSc, David B. Mandell, JD, MBA, Jason M. O'Dell, MS, CWM and Carole C. Foos, CPA

© 2013 Guardian Publishing, LLC Tel: (877) 656-4362

THIS PUBLICATION IS DESIGNED TO PROVIDE ACCURATE AND AUTHORITATIVE INFORMATION IN REGARD TO THE SUBJECT MATTER COVERED. IT IS SOLD WITH THE UNDERSTANDING THAT THE PUBLISHER IS NOT ENGAGED IN RENDERING LEGAL, ACCOUNTING, OR OTHER PROFESSIONAL SERVICES. IF LEGAL ADVICE OR OTHER EXPERT ASSISTANCE IS REQUIRED, THE SERVICE OF A COMPETENT PROFESSIONAL PERSON SHOULD BE SOUGHT.

—From a Declaration of Principles jointly adopted by a Committee of the American Bar Association and a Committee of Publishers.

ISBN: 978-0-9965569-5-8
Manufactured in the United States of America.

About The Authors

Peter J. Millett, MD, MSc

Dr. Peter J. Millett is an orthopaedic surgeon and partner at the internationally renowned Steadman Clinic in Vail, Colorado. Prior to coming to Vail, Dr. Millett held a faculty appointment at Harvard Medical School and was formerly Co-Director of the Harvard Shoulder Service and the Harvard Shoulder Fellowship. While in Boston, he also founded and directed the Musculoskeletal Proteomics Research Group at Harvard, where his team discovered and patented the protein profile for osteoarthritis. His clinical practice in Boston was based at the prestigious Brigham & Women's and Massachusetts General Hospitals.

He has authored over 100 peer-reviewed, scientific articles, numerous book chapters, and two books on orthopaedics, sports medicine, and shoulder surgery. His academic work has been recognized with awards from several international societies, including the 2010 Achievement Award from the American Academy of Orthopaedic Surgeons for his contributions to the field.

Dr. Millett also serves as a shoulder and sports medicine consultant to the country of Bermuda and has treated elite athletes from the NFL, NBA, MLB, NHL, X-Games and Olympics. Board Certified by the American Board of Orthopaedic Surgery, Dr. Millett is also a member of numerous academic societies including the American Academy of Orthopaedic Surgeons, the American Shoulder and Elbow Surgeons, the American Orthopaedic Society for Sports Medicine, the Orthopaedic Research Society and the Arthroscopy Association of North America. Dr. Millett is also affiliated with the United States Ski and Snowboard Association and has served as a team physician for the U.S. Ski Team and as a consultant to the Montreal Canadiens, professional hockey club.

A native of Pennsylvania, Dr. Millett received his undergraduate degree from the University of Scranton, in Scranton, Pennsylvania and his medical degree from Dartmouth Medical School in Hanover, New Hampshire. He also studied as a research scholar at the University of Cambridge in England, where he was awarded a master's degree in science for his work in skeletal biology.

David B. Mandell, JD, MBA

David B. Mandell is a principal of OJM Group, attorney, author, and renowned authority in the fields of risk management, asset protection and financial planning. Mr. Mandell is co-author of the books *For Doctors Only: A Guide to Working Less* and state versions of the book for physicians in California, Ohio, Georgia and New York.

Mr. Mandell has also written two books for John Wiley & Sons, Inc., the oldest publisher in the U.S.: *Wealth Protection: Build & Preserve Your Financial Fortress* and *Wealth Secrets of the Affluent*. His previous books include *The Doctor's Wealth Protection Guide*, *Wealth Protection, MD* and the Category I CME Monograph *Risk Management for the Practicing Physician*, which continues today in its 6th printing.

Mr. Mandell has also published articles in more than 50 medical publications, and has addressed many of the nation's leading medical conferences, including the American Academy of Ophthalmology, the American Section of the International College of Surgeons, the American Association of Neurological Surgeons, the American Academy of Dermatology, the American Society of Plastic Surgeons, the American Society of Aesthetic Plastic Surgeons, and numerous others.

Mr. Mandell graduated with honors from Harvard University. His law degree is from the UCLA School of Law, where he was awarded the American Jurisprudence Award for achievement in legal ethics. While at UCLA, he also earned an MBA from the Anderson School of Management.

Jason M. O'Dell, MS, CWM

Jason M. O'Dell is a principal and managing partner of OJM Group with offices in Arizona, Florida, New York and Ohio. Mr. O'Dell is a co-author of the book *For Doctors Only: A Guide to Working Less & Building More* and *For Ohio Doctors: Shedding Light on Asset Protection, Tax & Estate Planning*. He has experience as an entrepreneur, financial consultant and investment advisor and has been working with high-net worth and physician clients for more than 20 years. Mr. O'Dell has conducted financial planning, asset protection and wealth management lectures throughout the nation and has been recognized by Medical Economics as "One of the Best Financial Advisers to Physicians" and by *Cincinnati Magazine* as a "Top Wealth Manager."

Mr. O'Dell graduated with a Bachelor of Arts in Economics from The Ohio State University and has earned a Master of Science degree with an emphasis in financial planning. He serves on the Board of Directors of the Alzheimer's Association of Greater Cincinnati and is a member of the Financial Planning Association, Cincinnati Estate Planning Council and the Advisory Board of Partners Financial.

Carole C. Foos, CPA

Carole Foos is an OJM Group principal and Certified Public Accountant (CPA) providing tax analysis and tax planning services to OJM clients. Carole is a co-author of several financial resources for physicians including *For Doctors Only: A Guide to Working Less & Building More*, *Wealth Protection Planning for Orthopaedic Surgeons and Sports Medicine Specialists* and the Category I CME Monograph *Risk Management for the Practicing Physician*. She has also authored numerous articles and presented lectures and web seminars on tax planning and financial topics.

Carole graduated with a BSBA from Xavier University in Accounting and has more than 20 years of experience in public accounting in the field of taxation. She was formerly a manager in the tax department of a Big 4 firm and spent several years in public accounting at local firms.

Over the course of her career, Carole has been a tax consultant to both individuals and businesses providing compliance and planning services, and currently maintains a tax practice in addition to her work with OJM.

Cheyenne Brinson, CPA, MBA

Cheyenne Brinson is a consultant with Karen Zupko & Associates (KZA) in Chicago. For over a decade, she has helped physician practices, ranging in size and specialties, solve business problems. She draws upon her experience as a CPA and her hands-on practice management experience to help surgeons across the country build solid internal controls, reduce overhead, reduce risk and increase revenue. Ms. Brinson works extensively with orthopaedic, plastic surgery, otolaryngology, neurosurgery, general surgery, and vascular surgery practices, from solo practices to group practices, to increase efficiencies for collections improvement and leverage overhead costs.

Ms. Brinson is also an instructor for KZA's national coding and reimbursement workshops sponsored by the American Academy of Orthopaedic Surgeons (AAOS) and the American Academy of Otolaryngology - Head and Neck Surgery Foundation (AAO-HNSF).

Ms. Brinson holds a Master's of Business Administration and Bachelor's degree in accounting from Troy State University (now Troy University) in Troy, Alabama. She is an inductee to the Accounting Hall of Honor in recognition of her professional accomplishments.

Table of Contents

Introduction

From Peter J. Millett, MD, MSc

As a busy surgeon, I know time is a physician's most valuable asset, and I appreciate and thank you for committing some of your time to reading our short book. I do think your time will be very well spent, as many of the warnings or insights I attempt to provide, as well as the solutions that my co-author experts explain, may have a significant impact on your long term financial well-being. In that vein, I would also like to quickly thank Jason and David for writing this book with me, along with Cheyenne Brinson for her contributions as well.

All of us experience the same feeling at some point, usually after a hectic day at the practice—where we think about how quickly time has passed since we were in medical school or fellowship.

"Can it really have been five, ten, or even 20 years since my first day at this practice?" This is a natural feeling. However, what is scarier than thinking about the time that has passed, is wondering about the plans you have made and how they will affect your future. "Have I planned—or planned well—for my financial future?"

For the first year or so in practice, we were happy to be earning "real" money after years living on a trainee's salary. As our practices grew, we saved a little and spent more, because that's what we're expected to do. Perhaps we even utilized an advisor or specialist to help us plan for the future.

Some of the planning may have helped and some may have been inadequate. Rarely was the planning as comprehensive as it needed to be, and rarely was it focused on our specific needs as an orthopaedic surgeon. We may have even made bad investments and lost money.

Because of the conflicts of interest that exist in the financial services industry, many physicians rightly feel that they are being sold a product or solution rather than being diagnosed and treated based on their particular circumstances. I can personally attest that I spent years looking for better advice in the fields of tax planning and asset protection before I felt that I was getting the proper advice my specific situation warranted.

Most of us face the same challenges. We start earning some money, buy a house, have a family, and try to save for our kids' education and for our own retirement. At the same time, we run a busy practice that absolutely demands most of our attention. We are highly trained in medicine, but not always in money matters. Most of us become high-income earners, yet at the end of the year we wonder where that income went. Unfortunately, we learn that most of our income comes to us as ordinary income—taxed at the highest level. We work the first five or six months of the year to pay Uncle Sam.

Furthermore, because of the nature of our profession, we also learn that we have significant exposure to lawsuits from malpractice and other business-related risks—especially for those of us who own our own practices.

We are all highly educated, yet we have little, if any, training in business skills, asset protection, tax, or retirement planning, and with our busy lives, we don't have the time to learn on our own. We not only fail to take advantage of strategies that could save us money, but many times we actually "invest" in risky strategies that end up not working out, losing money, or, worse—costing us money over and above our principal—simply to extricate ourselves from a bad situation.

Often times, simply out of inertia, we continue to use the same advisors that our family used, or that our neighbor recommended, or that we have kept since residency—even if the advisor hasn't really shown much value.

I know I have done this. As the old saying goes: *"We don't know what we don't know."* We typically do not have the skills or experience to examine our own tax returns, our wills, our asset protection planning, or our insurance products, and thus we don't know if we could do any better. We haven't been trained in these specialties, yet we often think we know what we need. As is the case in our field, I think it is important to consider second opinions and to be open to new strategies that are targeted to our needs.

The purpose of this book is to open your mind to different ideas and concepts. For many of you, this book will serve as a handbook of new approaches—not all of which will be new or appropriate for your current stage of life—but may be later. For others, this book may reinforce concepts that you are already aware of, but it may introduce you to more sophisticated strategies for building upon your existing structure.

In the following four sections, we will discuss issues that have become important in my own personal situation and in those of colleagues I know well. We will be the patients in this book and my co-authors will be the tertiary care specialists who will help us come up with the best diagnosis and treatment.

In each of the four sections, I will lay out specific challenges I have seen, and my co-authors, the specialists, will educate you on various "Lessons" to deal effectively with those challenges. They will share some of the best strategies to protect your assets, reduce your taxes, and plan for retirement, while at the same time offering suggestions on developing and growing your most important income producing asset—your orthopaedic or sports medicine practice.

You may find that certain strategies discussed are not right for your particular situation. That's natural, as not every doctor who reads this book is in the same situation. However, we do think it is useful to at least be aware of the various options that are available, so that an overall financial roadmap can be developed. Perhaps the planning and asset protection tools described herein, even if not useful today, may be of use in the future.

We hope this book will serve as a useful reference, a resource for tax planning, asset protection, and practice building. But we also hope it will be more. We hope that the book will not only get you thinking about financial planning and asset protection, but it will also serve as a call to action for planning your financial future. As the late, great coach John Wooden said, "Failing to plan is planning to fail."

So think carefully and take action so you can start planning for a financially sound future. Being goal-oriented orthopaedic surgeons, we know that if you can envision it, you can plan for it, and you can make it happen.

Again, thanks for your time and happy reading.

From David Mandell, JD, MBA, Jason O'Dell, MS, CWM and Carole Foos, CPA

We thank Peter for his invaluable contribution to this book, and we thank you for taking the time to read it. As Peter described, this book has been created in a "discuss challenge/discuss solutions" format. In each of the four areas, Peter will describe a particular challenge he has seen in practice or personal planning and we (along with consultant Cheyenne Brinson, CPA, MBA from Karen Zupko & Associates) will describe potential solutions to the challenge in our Lessons.

Our firm has worked with Peter for a number of years, and we have helped over 1,000 physicians of all specialties throughout the U.S. Our material in this book describes some of the ways we help our doctor clients every day. Some of the writing here is unique to this text, while some comes from our seven other books written over the years, starting with *The Doctor's Wealth Protection Guide* and the CME piece *Risk Management for the Practicing Physician* in 1998 and continuing to our latest book, *For Doctors Only: A Guide to Working Less & Building More.*

If anything in this book sparks your interest, we encourage you to contact us. We are always available for a free consultation to answer questions or to see how we might be able to help you, given your situation. You can reach us at *mandell@ojmgroup.com, odell@ojmgroup.com* or 877-656-4362.

What I've Learned About the Practice of Medicine

From Peter J. Millett, MD, MSc

One key lesson I have learned in my career is that, for many of us, in order to truly enjoy a rewarding career, we have to focus some of our time and energy on "business"–type issues, as well as clinical ones.

We live in uncertain times, particularly in medicine and orthopaedic surgery. New healthcare reform, lack of transparency in billing practices, and declining reimbursements all affect our present practice of medicine.

Most of us recognize these uncertainties, but we are too busy caring for patients to understand how the coming changes will influence us. We take a "wait and see" or reactionary approach— when often, a better approach would be to prepare and plan pro-actively. In general, most of us earn a good living, but I believe that through knowledge and education we can also prepare for a financially sound future.

For all the so–called bad news we hear every day, we also live in very exciting times. New technologies, new inventions, new procedures, and new treatments all allow us to provide better care for our patients with less invasive treatments, faster recoveries, and better outcomes. This is truly exciting and rewarding! Value–driven health care is the new norm, and tracking and improving our outcomes will be an important part of the new practice mandate.

As we prepare for these changes, there are other personal factors that we must consider:

1. How do we practice (solo, group, academic, hospital employee)?

2. How long will we practice?

3. How do we protect our assets in an era of increasing litigation?

4. How will we plan for our families and for the transfer of assets to our children?

5. What role will philanthropy and volunteerism play in our lives?

6. How will we save for retirement?

All of these factors play roles in our daily lives and affect our personal financial situation. In some cases, financial security often impacts our sense of happiness with our chosen field of profession.

At the heart of it, medicine remains an art and a science and the most rewarding of all careers. This is especially true in our field of medicine—orthopaedics and sports medicine—where the art and skill of the surgeon really impacts the outcome for the patients. We are the "captains of the ship," making important decisions for our patients each day.

Unfortunately, many of us don't often develop the same "captain of the ship" commitment to our own careers, our own practices, or our own families. We neglect to plan for ourselves and, as a result, we make bad decisions, or no decisions about where we are going or what we would like to accomplish.

One lesson I have learned is that the cliché of working only "in the business" instead of "on the business" applies to the practice of orthopaedic surgery as well. In this next section, David and Jason will give you some practical insights into how to be more proactive in your practice and your career.

Be the CEO of Your Career, Even if You are Employed

From David Mandell, JD, MBA, Jason O'Dell, MS, CWM
and Carole Foos, CPA

TRIAGE SUMMARY: You must act as the CEO of your own practice and career, and go beyond "seeing more patients" as a primary strategy. Learn how to use leverage—especially of your advisors and assets—and take advantage of the opportunities around you.

Work "On" Your Practice, Not Just "In" It

In medicine, patients come to physicians like you when their bodies are unable to heal themselves. Patients who delay seeking medical treatment are missing out on the power of modern medicine and failing to take advantage of an opportunity to dramatically improve their health. Similarly, the financial and legal ailments impacting your medical practice or personal finances cannot be healed without professional care. Simply working harder and hoping that the problems will solve themselves is like the patient hoping his body will heal itself.

Even more likely, you may not even see any problems yourself, but you will not be working at maximum efficiency without consulting an expert. You may think that you are adequately protected, pay the right amount of taxes, or are truly positioned well with your assets—but how do you know without a check–up or second opinion?

"Seeing More Patients"—A Placebo

Confronted with any legal, tax, or financial setback, many doctors follow the business strategy of "seeing more patients." If the practice suffers because of a successful lawsuit, a sudden unforeseen expense, or an unproductive associate, physicians often simply try to "make up for it" by seeing more patients in hopes of billing more—and orthopaedic surgeons follow the same instinct.

The same tactic is followed by many doctors who are behind in their retirement planning, who feel like they are paying too much in taxes, or who are getting divorced. Any financial setback seems to yield the same resulting behavior. Many physicians approach their entire career with the business strategy of working as long and as hard as possible for as long as they can physically endure it. Does this remind you of any of your peers? Do you see someone like this when you look in the mirror?

Certainly, there are many flaws to such a business strategy. Let's examine a few of these flaws so you can understand why other strategies are better:

1. **This strategy has diminishing financial returns**
   Even if you work harder and see more patients, each patient you see will potentially net you fewer dollars. As your marginal expenses for each additional hour of work may be the same and your taxes may increase if you hit new marginal tax levels, your "take home" may actually become less per dollar as you work harder. Even if this is not the case, the next two flaws certainly apply.

2. **This strategy has financial limits**
   Even if you worked as hard as you possibly could and you could make more on each additional dollar earned, you only have 24 hours per day. As a surgeon, do you really think that you can work 18 or 20 hours per day over an extended period of time? How long can you work without your skills suffering? Of course, you are capped in the total income that you can generate by "just seeing more patients."

3. **This strategy will take a great personal toll on you**
   Extreme stress, physical ailments, divorce, decreased life expectancy—these are all common symptoms for all physicians, and especially successful surgeons, who choose "seeing more patients" as their business mantra. Are these extreme personal costs worth it? We think not—especially given #4 below.

4. **There is a better way**
   If working as hard as you could was the only alternative available to allow you to meet your financial

goals, that would be one thing. However, the truth is that there is a much better concept upon which you can build your practice and personal finances. This concept will be explained below.

Use Leverage to Your Advantage

Let's consider the following all-too-common scenario. You work a very long day and generate $10,000 of billings. The insurance companies pay your practice $3,000 for your hard work. Your practice overhead is about 50%, so $1,500 of that income is gross profit. However, the $1,500 isn't yours. Of the $1,500 you actually receive, the Federal, state, and local tax authorities will take 40% to 50% or more in states like California or New York, leaving you with only $750 to $900. In other words, less than 10% of the work you do in a given day actually results in money you keep. This means that you have to do $3,000,000 worth of work in order to generate less than $300,000 of money for you to enjoy. Unless you want to continue to work ten times as hard as necessary, you have to learn to work smarter. This is the key to the concept of **Leverage**.

If you refer to the Merriam-Webster Dictionary and look up the word "Leverage," you will be presented with three definitions:

1. The action of a lever or the mechanical advantage gained by it;

2. POWER, EFFECTIVENESS;

3. The use of credit to enhance one's speculative capacity.

We will offer very simplified interpretations of the three definitions of Leverage stated above. The first definition states that Leverage increases the amount of force exerted. To exemplify this concept, think of Leverage as the act of wedging a stick between two heavy rocks that you could not move with just your hands. In order to efficiently move one of the rocks, you need to push down on the stick that you wedged between the rocks. In doing so, the rock can be moved. Leverage—the wedging of a stick— allows you to move a rock you would otherwise not be able to move.

The second definition of Leverage simply states that the act of Leverage allows people to be more efficient, effective, and powerful. This can be interpreted to mean that Leverage allows people to get more done in less time. It can also be interpreted to mean that Leverage allows people to get a job done with less effort. In either case, Leverage enables people to be more effective.

The third definition of Leverage applies to credit and loans. In this definition, Leverage allows people to buy things they don't have the money to buy in an effort for them to increase their financial capacity. To illustrate this definition, think of a home loan—the $500,000 home that is purchased by a family with only $100,000 of their own money to use as a down payment. Leverage is the ability to enjoy the use of or participate in the upside potential of an investment you otherwise could not afford.

Quite simply, Leverage is a method by which you can do more with less. Less effort. Less money. Less time. If you are looking for a shortcut to financial success, Leverage is the closest thing to it.

The Importance of Leverage

Successful physicians know that Leverage is an important tool to increase their wealth. Without Leverage, people would have to do everything themselves, including running their own business, earning money, handling financial affairs, paying for everything with only their own money, micromanaging everything at work and at home, and still finding time to eat and sleep.

If you feel like this is an accurate description of your life, then you are not using Leverage. Leverage makes your life easier. Leverage frees you to do the things that are most important, most profitable, or most enjoyable to you. Leverage is what allows you to achieve greater levels of financial success. No matter what your financial goals, mastering the art of Leverage and incorporating it into your planning will help you reach these goals faster. As we mentioned earlier, Leverage is how physicians can increase the power and effectiveness of their financial planning. You can do the same.

Financial Leverage: The Foundation of Wealth

For thousands of years, every great construction project required the use of levers to complete the building process. This was true for moving the large stones to build the pyramids of Egypt and lifting the stones for Stonehenge. Levers were used to build all of the great castles, churches, synagogues, and mosques around the world. Financial projects are very similar to construction projects. They can both seem overwhelming at the beginning, a collection of complex tasks that must be executed with skill and precision. The success of both types of projects begins with significant and detailed planning. After the plans are drawn, they must be implemented accordingly. One person alone could never accomplish the implementation of such plans. Instead, the plan requires a team of people working together to accomplish the same goal. For us, that goal is building and maintaining wealth.

Without exception, every high income earner and wealthy family has relied on financial Leverage in one way or another.

Once you grasp the concept of Leverage and the financial applications of Leverage, it becomes impossible to imagine how affluence could possibly be built without it.

Types of Financial Leverage

Physicians can use different types of financial Leverage to create and build wealth. These include:

Leverage of Effort: Since the goal of Leverage is to get more done with less effort, all forms of Leverage require that you leverage your individual effort by including the efforts of others.

Leverage of Assets: Leverage of assets is one way to increase your financial status and get more out of what you currently possess. If you had an unlimited amount of money or land, you wouldn't need to accumulate any more wealth; however, this is not the case for most people. Since we all have limited resources, we want to get the most wealth/asset accumulation and financial protection out of what we have with the least amount of effort and the lowest amount of risk.

Leverage of People: Savvy business owners know that they only have the capacity to do so much and that the Leverage of people is one way to get more than 24 hours out of a day. By leveraging other people's efforts, you can increase the number of tasks you can accomplish in a day. By leveraging people with special skills and expertise you don't possess, you can get things done in much less time than it would take you to do these same tasks, if you could accomplish them at all.

Generally speaking, physicians utilize Leverage to some degree, but they are not thorough in their application. They try to leverage effort by working hard; we know that. Doctors also may try to leverage assets in their practice through medical equipment for which they can bill and they may try to leverage people through technologists, nurses, and physician assistants, who can generate income to the practice. Still, few physicians apply this concept broadly enough in their practices to result in any real wealth building. Even fewer physicians effectively leverage people or assets with respect to their personal finances.

Leverage of Advisors: This is a sub-set of the "leverage of people" category, but it is important enough for us to break out. As advisors to over 1,000 physicians across the U.S., we see first-hand every day the benefits that can be gained by busy physicians if they have an expert coordinated advisor team working for them. This might come in the form of reduced income taxes, higher portfolio returns, better–protected assets, a superior corporate structure, better-leveraged benefit plans, a true retirement roadmap—or the psychological benefit to the doctor that they know they're well advised and do not have to be their own CFO, essentially, while also managing the practice and trying to have a life. What is this peace of mind quantifiably? For many busy surgeons, quite a bit.

Make Your Assets Work for You: The Power of Compound Interest

"Remember that money is of a prolific generating nature. Money can beget money, and its offspring can beget more." —*Benjamin Franklin*

"Compounding is mankind's greatest invention because it allows for the reliable, systematic accumulation of wealth." —*Albert Einstein*

We will start with some basics. At some point in your life, someone has undoubtedly explained to you the power of compound interest. Compound interest is a simple concept; your money makes money by virtue of interest earned on prior interest—which has become part of principal. In other words, the "compound" return is the subsequent return earned on earlier returns reinvested alongside the initial investment.

Compound interest is a simple way to build wealth—it just takes patience and discipline. You must have the patience to allow your money to grow on its own, and you must have the discipline to leave the money alone.

Let's take a look at a few examples that demonstrate the power of compound interest and how it affects retirement savings.

For our first set of examples, we will figure out what the annual contribution to a retirement fund would need to be in order to reach a goal of $1 million dollars by the age of 65. We will assume an annual rate of return of 6%, and we will assume for each age that the individual has already set aside a set amount in a fund.

These are basic examples. We are not factoring in taxes, inflation or any number of other factors that could affect any given specific situation. These examples are simply to put years and dollars into context for informational purposes only.

Current age	Retirement age	Expected annual return	Current amount saved in a fund	Goal	Annual Contribution Required
35	65	6%	$50,000	$1,000,000	$9,016.47
40	65	6%	$75,000	$1,000,000	$12,359.71
45	65	6%	$100,000	$1,000,000	$18,466.10
50	65	6%	$200,000	$1,000,000	$22,370.21
55	65	6%	$250,000	$1,000,000	$41,900.97
60	65	6%	$500,000	$1,000,000	$58,696.20

As you can see above, in the example of a 40-year-old with $75,000 in savings, who puts away $12,359.71 annually for 25 years, they save approximately $383,992.75 out of pocket.

$$12,359.71 \times 25 = 308,992.75 + 75,000 = 383,992.75$$

However, the 6% interest compounding over 25 years accounts for an additional $616,007.25, taking the individual to $1,000,000. The money earned via compound interest nearly doubled what the individual actually saved out of pocket.

$$383,992.75 + 616,007.25 = 1,000,000$$

Factoring In Inflation and Taxes

The above examples demonstrate the power of compound interest, but they do not tell the whole story. What happens when we account for two very real and important drags to real investment returns—taxes and inflation? What do you really have to save in order to reach your retirement goals? Also, if we want to look at saving to maintain a lifestyle in retirement, it is important that we calculate based on that—not just a stagnant lump sum at age 65.

In this way, if we factor in 3% inflation and a 30% tax rate, and assume now 7% returns, net of fees (a very generous assumption), and then calculate for an annual income requirement, you will see that you must save much more than previously calculated.

Below, we examine the annual required savings amounts for two basic levels of after-tax retirement wealth—$120,000 and

$240,000. In other words, if you think you can live comfortably on $10,000 per month after taxes today and want to project what you would need to save each year so that you can maintain that same lifestyle in *2013 dollars* when you get to age 65, look in the $120,000 column. If you require about $20,000 after-tax per month today and want to maintain that level of lifestyle in retirement, then the $240,000 is your column.

Age	Retirement Income Goal—in 2013 Dollars	Required Annual Savings— After-Tax	Retirement Income Goal— in 2013 Dollars	Required Annual Savings— After-Tax
35	$120,000	$66,748	$240,000	$132,956
40	$120,000	$79,387	$240,000	$158,774
45	$120,000	$97,993	$240,000	$195,986
50	$120,000	$127,627	$240,000	$255,254
55	$120,000	$183,328	$240,000	$366,657

Keep in mind, there is no guarantee returns will be 7% post-fee—in fact, that is a very generous assumption. Of course, as returns decrease, savings must increase to make up for it. Should returns creep into the 3-4% range for a period of time, you may have to double your actual savings to reach your goals. Also, if returns decrease, you will have to fight the urge to increase your risk tolerance just to make up for it—especially as you get older and closer to retirement.

As you can see above, there are some significant savings requirements here. While we assume $0 other savings to get you to the goal and you may have some (real estate equity, etc.), this underscores the need for a well-modeled, comprehensive financial plan. As Peter quoted Coach John Wooden saying, "Failing to plan is a plan to fail."

Accumulating and sustaining wealth during volatile markets is not easy. There are different ways to build wealth in up, down, and sideways markets that go beyond socking money away, diversification, and managing risk. We will discuss some of these later in this book.

See Opportunities Around You

Many orthopaedic surgeons and sports medicine specialists already recognize the many opportunities to become a "doctrepreneur" in the enormous healthcare business space.

If you haven't yet seriously looked at your position in the healthcare system as a source for wealth creation, now is the time. Spending on healthcare in the U.S. in 2010 accounted for 17.6% of the Gross Domestic Product.[1] With an estimated $2.7 trillion spent on healthcare expenditures in the U.S. in 2011 and projections for 2016 reaching $3.6 trillion, it is obvious that there are opportunities all around you.[2] Here are a few to consider:

Real Estate: One way to get started leveraging your practice to create more wealth is to consider the physical location of your practice. Would it make more sense to own the building rather than leasing space? If you owned the building, could you also rent space to others? Investing in commercial real estate may seem daunting, but it can provide for reliable streams of additional income.

Ambulatory Surgery Centers (ASC): Getting involved in or starting a surgery center provides physicians the opportunity to pool services, increase efficiency, get higher percentages of reimbursement for procedures, and obtain higher profits with the same working hours. Many centers help doctors increase the quality of care and decrease overall costs to patients. Baby boomers demand relief from their ailments, be it a joint replacement or treatment for an injury. They typically seek out "one-stop shops" and treatment options that call for the shortest possible recovery time and the lowest possible out-of-pocket costs. Catering to the aging boomer population could be a lucrative endeavor.

Medical Devices: As more than 70 million boomers hit retirement age in the coming years, you can expect medical device sales and development to continue to rise—despite a 2.3% tax on medical devices that began in 2013.[3] Indeed, by 2030 an estimated 4

---

[1] Statistics taken from the Centers for Medicare & Medicaid Services, Office of the Actuary, National Health Statistics Group.

[2] *Id.*

3 Section 4191 of Internal Revenue Code—effective December 31, 2012.

million knees will need to be replaced in the U.S. alone.[4] With an aging population and an improving economy, the government is projecting spending on medical services to reach nearly 20% of the U.S. gross domestic product by 2021.[5]

As frontline participants in the ever-expanding field of healthcare, you have the ability to realize opportunities before others and get involved early. Stay cognizant of what is going on in your field. Stay alert to opportunities. Don't be afraid of change—be prepared take advantage of innovation to make your practice more profitable. Always seek out ways to make your line of business work for you.

4 *Projections of Primary and Revision Hip and Knee Arthopasty in the U.S from 2005 to 2030*; The Journal of Bone and Joint Surgery, American Volume; 2007 Apr,89 (4): 780-5; S. Kurtz; K. Ong; E. Lau; F. Mowat; and M. Halpern

5 Statistics taken from the Centers for Medicare & Medicaid Services, Office of the Actuary, National Health Statistics Group

The Risks of Practicing Medicine & How to Protect Yourself

From Peter J. Millett, MD, MSc

As you likely know by now, the practice of medicine brings with it a host of risks, especially for us surgeons. The risks are especially heightened for those of us in private practice. I'll give you my thoughts on a few areas that I have seen create risk and liability over the years—for my practice, colleagues, friends, and family.

HIPAA

If you are not careful, HIPAA laws in effect can create traps. In fact, there was a doctor I know who had a HIPAA breach. The patient actually filed a lawsuit against him. I was also involved in a HIPAA-related claim.

In our situation, a disgruntled employee whom I had seen for a workers' compensation injury accused our practice of an alleged HIPAA violation because we shared the patient's records with the employer's attorneys. The rule under these circumstances is that an employer is permitted to receive all documentation, so it wasn't a breach. Still, the claim opened my eyes to the seriousness of the HIPAA-related issues. I had to file a response with the state board because of the accusation. And while my practice was completely absolved, it nevertheless made me realize how easily a breach could occur. It also forced me to recognize the litigious environment we all practice in.

Obviously, HIPAA violations must be taken seriously as a real category of risk that can impact our practices. Ignorance is not an excuse—we have to be familiar with what appropriate patient protection is, and what it is not. Of course, this may add to the overhead burden of the practice and impact profitability, but you must have compliance officers and you need to do appropriate auditing within your own practice. If you have the right checks and balances in place, it can help mitigate things if there is a breach.

Employee Liability

One area that varies from state to state is employment law. In Colorado, where I practice, this is not as big an issue as in other states because Colorado is an "at will" employment state. This means employers like medical practices have more leeway to fire people than in other states, where wrongful termination lawsuits are more common. I know some colleagues who have had to deal with these types of lawsuits, and I have heard their horror stories.

We all want to avoid these headaches. And as is the case with medicine, consulting an expert in the field sooner rather than later is always recommended. The experts will tell you that documentation is key—similar to medical record keeping.

It seems like common sense, but if you have an employee who is not performing at their appropriate level, I think it is always advisable to document their deficiencies and performance. This is important so that when you do eventually terminate them, you have a paper trail demonstrating the rationale and reasoning for the termination. Getting appropriate guidance by an employment attorney should always be part of the plan.

Malpractice

Malpractice is something that concerns me, as it does most physicians in all specialties. Luckily, I have only been named in one lawsuit, which involved Vioxx. My patient was taking Vioxx for a separate issue unrelated to what I was treating her for. She had a simple knee arthroscopy, but afterwards she resumed Vioxx. Then several weeks later, she developed a GI bleed that her attorney attributed to the medication. All the doctors and hospitals that had ever cared for her were named in the suit.

Fortunately, after I wrote a report for my attorney and spent weeks agonizing about the case, the lawsuit was found to be meritless and the case was dropped.

However, I remember how I felt when I was notified of the

lawsuit. My stomach sank and I felt awful about it. In addition to the extra time it took away from my family and my practice, and the stress of thinking about a worst case scenario in a lawsuit, I also didn't like the feeling of being financially exposed to a lawsuit—even a meritless suit.

The suit motivated me to find out more about asset protection planning as an additional "insurance" plan against a worst case scenario.

What should you do regarding malpractice claims? I think the most important thing is to try to prevent it in the first place, by practicing within the standard of care for your profession, by maintaining your technical proficiency, by maintaining your certification and continuing medical education, and by developing excellent communication skills. If you are trying a new procedure, tell the patient the risks and clearly inform them ahead of time.

Should something adverse happen, deal with it as soon as possible. As one of my mentors said, "When you spot trouble, get close to it." Call the patient, see the patient more frequently, be available to speak on the phone, and then carefully document everything you do. Patients and juries understand that what we do is not a perfect science. You will, however, find little understanding if you do not communicate with your patient or properly document the treatment plan.

I have served as an expert witness in a number of cases, and I have seen the same pattern over and over again. First an adverse outcome occurs, followed by a breakdown in communication with some, but not adequate, documentation. If the case comes to trial, without proper documentation, it becomes a "he said, she said" scenario—one that is much more difficult to defend.

Asset Protection

Asset protection planning is very important in our profession. It is more important in certain regions of the country where litigation is more prevalent. For example, I am from Pennsylvania, a state where a few years ago malpractice litigation became so prevalent that orthopaedic surgeons had a hard time getting appropriate malpractice coverage at reasonable rates. Even today, in states like Florida, some physicians choose not to carry malpractice insurance because of the cost. Obviously, these physicians have to shield themselves with planning beyond insurance.

Even though one might have malpractice coverage at a reasonable rate, I don't think that is enough. Remember, malpractice coverage has limits to it (and exclusions). For those of us who handle high–profile clients, professional athletes or other prominent patients, a poor outcome and an adverse judgment could result in damages that could go well beyond what insurance will provide.

We are also exposed to business risks as practice-owners and small businessmen. Many of these additional risks are not covered by malpractice. Risks like employment issues, small business liabilities, and HIPAA or Medicare violations all need to be considered and ideally insured against. But gaps in coverage and the potential for exposure that exceeds your coverage limits makes asset protection crucial.

The bottom line is none of us wants to be sued, but it could happen—and for some it may happen more than once. It is very stressful to be named in a lawsuit and it creates a lot of personal tension. Your personal integrity, your ability, your judgment, and your professionalism all come into question, and it is easy to get distracted. By having a good plan in place before you have a problem, you know that if something happens, your home, your investments, your retirement, and your education funds will be protected, so that your financial future will be stable no matter what happens.

Disability

Disability insurance is critical for a sound financial plan. I know of several surgeons who have become disabled and could no longer earn an income. One of my co-residents during my training became disabled when he slipped on a wet floor, suffered a head injury, and was permanently unable to operate. Unfortunately, he was also at a stage of his career where he could not yet obtain a good disability policy because his income as a resident was too low to justify an adequate policy.

It is important, particularly for younger physicians, to get adequate disability insurance. Your biggest risk is the potential loss of earning power through injury or illness. When you are early in your career, you are healthy and your practice starts to ramp up—that is the time to get a very good disability policy and try to get the maximum you can afford or the maximum coverage allowable. It is important to think about this when you are in your 30s because as we age, we are more susceptible to developing health problems that could affect our ability to practice medicine. Whether it's an orthopaedic issue, a problem with your vision, a neurologic condition, or some other ailment (all of which I have seen in my colleagues), there are health risks that could affect one's ability to practice orthopaedic surgery. Many of these conditions we don't think about when we are young, yet they can pose significant risk to our livelihood.

Most orthopaedic surgeons and sports medicine doctors lead pretty active lifestyles (skiing, cycling, surfing, driving race cars, or flying planes). Couple this activity with the stress and long hours of practicing surgery, and it becomes apparent how important it is to obtain a good disability policy. A disability that keeps us from working is probably our greatest personal financial risk. Disability can come from injury or illness and at any time. In my opinion, a good disability insurance plan is an extremely important cornerstone of any surgeon's financial plan.

Protect What You Have

David Mandell, JD, MBA, Jason O'Dell, MS, CWM
and Carole Foos, CPA

TRIAGE SUMMARY: There are a variety of tools that can shield practice assets, cash flow, and personal wealth from potential lawsuits. We discuss their asset protection effectiveness in terms of a (-5) to (+5) sliding scale and examine just a few in depth here—especially those tools that can also help you reduce taxes and build wealth. We also examine the specific issues around divorce protection and protecting income against disability.

The Sliding Scale
of Asset Protection

The most common misconception among all doctors, including orthopaedic surgeons, regarding asset protection is the idea that an asset is either "protected" or "unprotected." This black or white analysis is no more accurate in the field of asset protection than it is in the field of medicine. In fact, asset protection advisors are very similar to physicians in how they approach any client or patient. In this chapter, we will discuss the way in which advisors measure a client's assets by using a sliding scale. Then we will suggest ways in which orthopaedic surgeons can protect assets, avoid high-risk assets, and achieve a high level of protection.

The Sliding Scale and Scores

To measure the assets of a client, advisors use a sliding scale that indicates the client's good and bad financial habits. Like doctors, asset protection professionals will first try to get a client to avoid bad habits. For a medical patient, bad habits might mean smoking, drinking too much, or maintaining a poor diet. For a client of ours, bad habits might include owning property in their own name, owning property jointly with a spouse, or failing to maximize the percentage of exempt assets in an investment portfolio.

Like a surgeon who judges the severity of a patient's illness, asset protection specialists use a rating system to determine the protection or vulnerability of a client's particular asset. The sliding scale runs from −5 (totally vulnerable) to +5 (superior protection). As you have probably already guessed, our goal is to bring a client's score closer to (+5) for each of their assets (see diagram below).

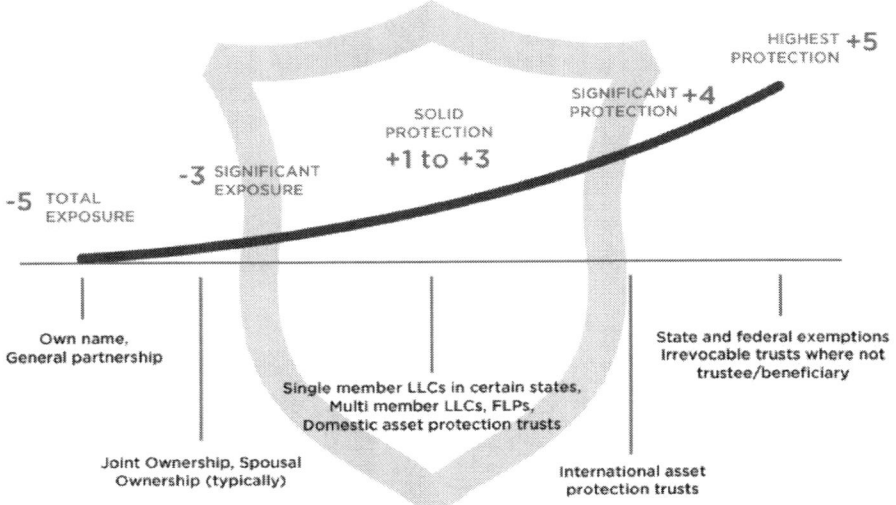

*The scale presumes tools are created and utilized properly and when fraudulent transfer rules will not apply.

When most clients initially come to see us, their asset planning scores are overwhelmingly on the negative side of the scale. The reason for this score varies. Typically, personal assets are owned jointly (-3) or in their individual name (-5). Both of these ownership forms provide little protection from lawsuits and may also have negative tax and estate planning implications.

Many medical practices themselves also have asset planning scores that are overwhelming negative. For practices, the worst way to operate a business or title assets is a general partnership (-5). For all other business entities, liability from operations is always a concern. For this reason, owning any business assets within an operating business is extremely unwise (-5).

Before asset protection specialists can achieve a high level of protection for their clients, they must first eliminate the high risk assets. There are many ways to protect assets, but the most efficient way to avoid high risk assets and achieve a high level of protection is to utilize exempt assets. This is mentioned briefly in the next section and then discussed in greater detail later in the Lesson.

The Best Protection:
Federal and State Exempt Assets

Each state's law identifies assets that are absolutely exempt from creditor claims in that state. Federal law also exempts certain assets. Because these assets are inherently protected by law, they enjoy the highest level of protection, a (+5) score on the sliding scale.

At the federal level, bankruptcy law affords (+5) protection for qualified retirement plans, such as pensions and 401(k) plans. At the state level, the rules vary widely between states. Please contact us to discuss how your state may shield certain assets as exempt (+5).

Basic Domestic Legal Tools

In many states, the list of state exemptions is not very generous. Even in those states where the exemptions are broad, we need to make sure that the asset protection goals are balanced with wealth accumulation and investment goals. For these reasons, there will almost always be non-exempt assets in a client's asset mix. For these assets, we must use other protection tools.

In such a situation, the basic asset protection tools are family limited partnerships (FLPs), limited liability companies (LLCs), and certain types of trusts. FLPs and LLCs provide good to excellent asset protection against future lawsuits, allow you to maintain control, and can provide income and estate tax benefits in certain situations. Trusts are quite varied in their ability to protect assets and factors in terms of tax treatment and access, but there are many solid options as well. For these reasons, we call FLPs and LLCs (and to some degree, trusts) the building blocks of a basic asset protection plan.

FLPs and LLCs (and properly structured trusts) afford asset protection scores somewhere between (+1) to (+4), depending on the circumstances. It may be possible to increase these scores for some of your assets by employing the laws of other states to protect them.

Other Protection Strategies

Most orthopaedic surgeons can achieve most of their asset protection planning with a combination of exempt assets and legal tools like FLPs, LLCs, and certain types of trusts. However, specialists who are worth more than $3,000,000, or who earn more than $500,000, almost always need additional planning strategies to help them protect their assets. More successful orthopaedic surgeons may utilize advanced techniques like:

Non-Qualified/Hybrid Plans

Certain Non-Qualified or Hybrid Benefit Plans used in a medical practice may provide asset protection benefits vis-à-vis creditors of the physician. In addition, these tools can offer tax-deferral and estate planning benefits. Most doctors find these tools attractive because employees need not be covered in these plans to be successful.

Captive Insurance Companies

Captive Insurance Companies can also reach the (+5) status when the shares are owned by a second entity like an irrevocable trust. Successful businesses can use such insurance companies to provide superior asset protection and risk management, efficiently fund a partner buy-out, and potentially reduce income and estate taxes.

Debt Shields and Collateralization

Debt Shield and Collateralization strategies are ideal for protecting equity in real estate, especially the personal residence and the medical practice's Accounts Receivable (AR). This technique helps achieve a (+1) to (+5) rating. The exact score depends on the funding vehicles used in this technique. When structured properly, after-tax wealth can be built while protecting the real estate equity or Accounts Receivable in a superior way.

The Diagnosis

Asset protection planning, like any sophisticated multi-disciplinary effort, has degrees of success. Nothing in life is 100% certain (except perhaps death and taxes—both of which are discussed in depth in our book *For Doctors Only*). For asset protection planning, this adage holds true. You can protect each personal or practice asset to different levels. Exempt assets offer the greatest level of protection with the least cost. Legal tools generally fill in the rest of the plan for many orthopaedic surgeons. Successful surgeons may choose to add Debt Shields, Captive Insurance Companies, or Non-Qualified/Hybrid Plans to complete the planning.

In your asset protection plan, make sure you understand the benefits and consequences of the various tools you employ. Your asset protection advisor can help you weigh the pros and cons of each potential strategy. Your advisory team can help explain how each asset protection strategy or tool may be integrated into your comprehensive financial plan. By addressing your asset protection concerns as part of a comprehensive planning process, you will not only protect the wealth you have already built, but you may find more efficient ways to build greater after-tax wealth for your retirement and for future generations.

Maximizing Exempt Assets

In the following chapters, we will explain a number of legal entities and techniques we use to protect the assets of our physician clients. This chapter on maximizing exempt assets precedes the following chapters because, in our view, clients should always maximize their use of exempt assets before moving on to legal tools, legal entities, and other techniques.

Despite their superiority to other asset protection strategies, most orthopaedic surgeons do not adequately use exempt assets. This chapter will explain why many advisors don't recommend exempt assets as often as they should. Then we will discuss all of the exempt assets that can be valuable components of a comprehensive financial plan and how sophisticated doctors save time and money by leveraging exempt assets that offer additional benefits. For now, let's begin discussing why exempt assets are considered the best asset protection tool and then discuss the reasons why they remain underutilized in asset protection planning.

Exempt Assets:
The Best Asset Protection Tools

We consider exempt assets to be the best asset protection tool for the following reasons:

1. **No legal/accounting/state fees.** Most of the tools in subsequent chapters, such as FLPs, LLCs, and trusts, involve the creation of legal entities that require set–up and ongoing legal fees, state fees, accounting

fees, and even additional taxes. Using the exempt assets described in this chapter involves **none of these significant costs** and affords better protection as well.

2. **No loss of ownership or control.** The legal tools of the following chapters typically require giving up some level of ownership or control to family members or even third-party trustees. **By using exempt assets, you can own and access the asset at any time while enjoying the highest (+5) level of protection.**

3. **Superior Protection.** The legal tools explained later offer protection that ranges from (+1) to (+5). Exempt assets always enjoy the top (+5) protection up to their exempt amount.

Why Exempt Assets Are Underutilized

Given the clear benefits of exempt assets, one would think that exempt assets would be preferred over other tools in an asset protection plan. Surprisingly, this is often not the case. The reason for this may be that most asset protection planning is implemented by an attorney who is not familiar with the financial tools a multi-disciplinary team could offer.

There are various planning pitfalls that can arise when you do not have the benefit of a coordinated, multi-disciplinary team to help implement your plan. Attorneys generally do not understand many of the exempt asset classes, such as cash value life insurance and annuities. You cannot expect an advisor to recommend something he doesn't understand.

This doesn't mean that one attorney could not recommend an adequate asset protection plan. What it does mean is that the plan created by one attorney may not be efficient, because the plan may be limited only to legal solutions. If you were more skeptical, you might point out that attorneys are generally not licensed to sell such financial products. Is it unrealistic to expect an attorney to have a bias against the use of exempt assets for asset protection when the implementation of those assets does not require any legal work?

Is it unreasonable to expect attorneys to focus their asset protection recommendations around the use of legal documents that may generate thousands of dollars in legal fees? This is not a conspiracy against, nor is it an indictment of, attorneys; we, as an author group, include an attorney —David. However, we appreciate multi-disciplinary planning and recognize the value of financial, as well as legal, solutions. **The reason our firm employs attorneys, CPAs, insurance, benefit, and investment experts is that we believe 100% in a multi-disciplinary approach to asset protection planning.**

The lesson here is simple. Your asset protection plan, like the rest of your financial plan, MUST be handled by a coordinated, multi-disciplinary team that carefully considers all planning options to help you efficiently achieve your goals. The absence of exempt assets in a plan is always a warning sign that the planning is not coordinated.

Federally Exempt Assets and the 2005 Bankruptcy Act (BAPCPA)

Federally exempt assets are those assets that are protected under federal bankruptcy law. In 2005 Congress enacted the Bankruptcy Abuse Prevention and Consumer Protection Act (BAPCPA), which brought about sweeping changes to debtor and creditor law. Federal law protects certain assets from creditors and lawsuits if the defendant is willing to file bankruptcy to eliminate the creditor.

BAPCPA and the U.S. Bankruptcy Code generally allow individual debtors to exempt certain property from creditor claims based on exemptions under either federal law or state law. Exemptions vary from state to state. Each state is permitted by the Bankruptcy rules to adopt its own set of bankruptcy exemptions to be used in place of the federal exemptions.

Two significant asset classes that federal law protects are qualified retirement plans (QRPs) and most IRAs. The term "qualified" retirement plan means that the retirement plan complies with certain Department of Labor and Internal Revenue Service rules. You might know such plans by their specific type, including profit sharing plans, money purchase plans, 401(k)s, or 403(b)s. Most IRAs are very similar to such plans, with several technical differences, and for the most part (with a couple of exceptions) are now given exempt status under the federal law as well.

While this protection is (+5), you must recognize that this federal protection only applies if you are in a bankruptcy setting. If you were simply sued and a creditor was trying to take the funds in your pension or IRA, bankruptcy protection would not apply. You would have to take the step of filing for bankruptcy to shield the asset. This might be too great a cost for the protection.

If you do not file for bankruptcy, this federal bankruptcy protection would not apply. However, the amount of value in any type of asset class that would be protected would depend on state law.

If you do not file for bankruptcy, this federal protection would not apply. The amount of value in the QRP or IRA that would be protected outside of bankruptcy would be controlled by state law. While many states do provide the same (+5) shield for QRPs and IRAs, not all do.

To understand the level of protection of QRPs and IRAs in your state, contact us at www.ojmgroup.com. We work collaboratively with attorneys in every state on our planning with clients.

State Exempt Assets

State exemption leveraging is a fundamental part of a financial plan and one which every orthopaedic surgeon should take seriously. The most significant state exemptions are:

1. Qualified Retirement Plans (QRPs) and Individual Retirement Accounts (IRAs)

2. Primary Residence (or Homestead)

3. Life Insurance

4. Annuities

Important Note: We will make general comments regarding state exemptions below. If you want to know how your state exemptions work, please call us at 877-656-4362.

Qualified Retirement Plans and IRAs

Outside of bankruptcy, any protection for QRPs or IRAs would be provided by state law. Most states provide (+5) protection for QRPs. Fewer states shield IRAs at a (+5) level. For IRAs, a number of states will only protect "the amount reasonably necessary for support," leaving it up to a judge to decide how much should be shielded in any particular case. While this may be adequate for most people who generally have not accumulated much in such accounts, it certainly will not provide a shield for the IRAs of most sports medicine physicians.

Primary Residence: Homestead

Many physicians consider the home to be their family's most valuable asset—from a purely economic perspective or psychologically. You may have thought you knew the laws that protect your home. Perhaps you have previously heard the term "homestead," and assumed that you could never lose your home to bad debts or other liabilities because of this homestead protection. The reality is that few states provide a total (+5) shield for the home.

Most states only protect between $10,000 and $60,000 of the homestead's equity. Some states, such as New Jersey, provide no protection, while other states, such as Florida and Texas, provide unlimited protection (with some restrictions). Given today's real estate values and the equity that many orthopaedic surgeons have in their homes, it is clear that most states' homestead exemptions provide inadequate protection.

To determine how well a homestead law protects your home, you should compare the protected value to the equity. In order to do so, subtract the value of any mortgages from the fair market value of your home. For example, if you live in a home with a $300,000 fair market value and have a $150,000 mortgage, then your equity is $150,000. If your state protects only $20,000 through its homestead law, then you still have $130,000 ($150,000 of equity—$20,000 homestead) of vulnerable equity.

Homestead protection is often automatic, but may require additional action in some cases. Each state has specific requirements for claiming homestead status. In some states, you must file a declaration of homestead in a public office. Other states set a time requirement for residency before homestead protection is granted. Never assume your home is protected. You may be wrong, and your inaction may cost you the protection you deserve. Your asset protection advisor can show you how to comply with the formalities in your state.

Life Insurance: Protected Everywhere

All 50 states have laws that protect varying amounts of life insurance. For example:

- Many states shield the entire policy proceeds from the creditors of the policyholder. Some also protect against the beneficiary's creditors.

- States that do not protect the entire policy proceeds set amounts above which the creditor can take proceeds.

- Many states protect the policy proceeds only if the policy beneficiaries are the policyholder's spouse, children, or other dependents.

- Some states protect a policy's cash value in addition to the policy proceeds. This can be the most valuable exemption opportunity.

One of the reasons for the under-utilization of life insurance as an exempt asset is that most clients—and advisors—do not understand the financial value of cash value life insurance. If they did, they would use it more often as a wealth accumulation and protection tool.

Annuities: Shielded in Many States

Another exempt asset in many states is the annuity. Annuities are insurance contracts that offer the upside of investment appreciation, tax-deferred growth, and principal protection. This diverse list of benefits makes annuities important components of asset protection and wealth accumulation plans.

As with life insurance, the amount of protection varies widely throughout the states, from total (+5) protection to an unlimited value to no shield whatsoever.

The Diagnosis

The easiest and most effective way to achieve the highest level of asset protection is to use exempt assets. For this reason, it makes sense that every orthopaedic surgeon who is interested in asset protection should attempt to maximize his or her use of exempt assets. However, to use exempt assets properly within a comprehensive financial plan, you may need an insurance product, home loan, qualified plan, and tax and asset protection expertise. This is another example of why you need a multi-disciplinary team to help you achieve your financial goals.

Practically, because asset protection is just one goal of a comprehensive plan (along with wealth accumulation, retirement planning, cash flow planning, liquidity concerns, etc.), we never recommend that a client place every dollar of their wealth into exempt assets—in fact, far from it. For this reason, you will have to utilize legal strategies as part of your asset protection planning. The following chapter will discuss the most common asset protection tools: the Family Limited Partnership and the Limited Liability Company.

Family Limited Partnerships and Limited Liability Companies

While (+5) exempt assets may be the most effective asset protection tools, most clients will need to go beyond the use of exempt assets in their quest to protect assets. They will make use of legal tools as well. Of all the legal tools we use to shield assets, the two we use most are Family Limited Partnerships (FLPs) and Limited Liability Companies (LLCs). Of course, having family members play a role in these tools is common—that's why we use the "F" in front of the "LP." However, using family members in this way is NOT required. Whether you use family members or non-family members, these entities can provide you solid asset protection. In this chapter we will discuss the similarities of the two tools, how they protect assets, and three tactics doctors should use to incorporate FLPs and LLCs into their plans to build and preserve wealth.

FLPs and LLCs: Similarities and Differences

We have combined FLPs and LLCs in this chapter because they are very similar. You can think of them as closely related, like brothers and sisters, as they share many of their best characteristics. In fact, unless we make the point otherwise, we will use these tools interchangeably: If a case study refers to an FLP, you can generally assume that an LLC could have been used and *vice versa*. Similarities between the FLP and LLC include:

1. **They are both legal entities certified under state law.** Both FLPs and LLCs are legal entities governed by the state law in the state in which the entity is

formed. Many of these laws are identical, as they are modeled after the Uniform Limited Partnership and Limited Liability Company Acts, which have been adopted at least partially by every state. As state-certified legal entities, state fees must be paid each year to keep an FLP or LLC valid.

2. **They both have two levels of ownership.** FLPs and LLCs allow for two levels of ownership. We'll call one ownership level "active ownership"—that is, the active owners have 100% control of the entity and its assets. In the FLP, the active owners are called "general partners," while in the LLC the active owners are called "managing members." (Note Well: Managers of LLCs do not have to be "owners.")

As you may have guessed, the second ownership level is "passive ownership"—the passive owners have little control over the entity and only limited rights. The passive owners are called "limited partners" in the FLP and "members" in the LLC.

This bi-level structure of ownership allows a host of planning possibilities because clients can use FLPs and LLCs to share ownership with family members without having to give away any practical control. Why is it optimal to be able to give away ownership but still maintain control? Asset protection reasons will be discussed in great detail in this chapter and estate planning benefits will be explained in Chapter 9-5.

3. **They both have beneficial tax treatment.** In terms of income taxes, both tools can elect for "pass through" taxation, meaning neither the FLP nor the LLC is liable for income taxes. Rather, the tax liability for any and all income or capital gains on FLP/LLC assets "passes through" to the owners (partners or members). Also, as discussed in the income tax and estate planning Lessons, both entities allow the participants to take advantage of "income sharing" and "valuation discount" techniques in the same ways.

Two Differences Between the FLP and LLC

1. **Only the LLC can be used for a single owner.** Most states now allow single-member (owner) LLCs, while a limited partnership in every state must have at least two owners. Thus, for single clients, the LLC is often the only option. However, there have been a number of recent legal decisions that have weakened the liability protections provided by one-person LLCs. The formation of a one-person LLC needs to be reviewed in light of these recent court decisions and should be set up, if possible, in one of the states that has superior statutory protections for single-owner LLCs.

2. **The FLP's general partner has liability for the FLP.** While a general partner has personal liability for the acts and debts of the FLP, a managing member has no such liability for his/her LLC. For this reason alone, asset protection experts always recommend using an LLC rather than an FLP when the entity will own "dangerous" assets —i.e., those likely to lead to lawsuits.

   "Safe" assets, conversely, are those that are unlikely to lead to lawsuits. Common safe assets include cash, stocks, bonds, mutual funds, CDs, life insurance policies, checking or savings accounts, antiques, artwork, jewelry, licenses, copyrights, trademarks, and patents, among others.

   "Dangerous" assets are those that have a relatively high likelihood of creating liability. Common dangerous assets include real estate (especially rental real estate), cars, RVs, trucks, boats, airplanes, and interests in closely held businesses.

How FLPs and LLCs Protect Assets and the Emerging Trends for FLPs and LLCs

The discussion of this section assumes that, in transferring assets to an FLP or LLC, you do not run afoul of fraudulent transfer laws. We discussed these laws in the introduction of this Lesson. It also assumes that one remains in compliance with state laws and does not use the FLP/LLC as an alter ego of one's personal business affairs.

This section will review in particular: (1) the general asset protection rules (including a brief legislative history) of FLPs and LLCs, (2) the charging order remedy, (3) the practical effect of the charging order protections offered by FLPs and LLCs, (4) the emerging trends of asset protection for FLPs and LLCs, (5) judicial foreclosure of LLC or FLP interest, and (6) the options available for debtors regarding FLP and LLC asset protection.

1. **The General Asset Protection Rules for FLPs and LLCs.** As a general rule, FLPs and LLCs are fairly good asset protectors because the law (both statutory law and judicial case law) prescribes the specific remedies which creditors are permitted to exercise when coming after assets in either entity. The legislative basis for the FLP laws in most states comes from the 1976 and 2001 Revised Uniform Limited Partnership Act (RULPA).

   Similarly, there is a Uniform Limited Liability Company Act for LLCs, but most states have not followed this Act, and instead have drafted their own LLC laws. However, when it comes to creditors' rights, many of the LLC laws in these states have adopted the 1976 RULPA concepts, so the creditor remedies for LLCs and FLPs are very similar. When a personal creditor pursues you and your assets are owned by an FLP or LLC, the creditor typically cannot seize the assets in the FLP/LLC. Under the limited partnership laws (governing FLPs) and LLC laws of several states, a creditor of a partner (or LLC member) cannot reach into the FLP/LLC and take specific partnership assets.

2. **The Charging Order Remedy for FLPs and LLCs.** Creditors can generally force the liquidation of corporations, but not so for an FLP or LLC. If the creditor cannot seize FLP/LLC assets, what can the

creditor get? The law normally allows a unique remedy: the "charging order." A charging order is something a creditor can obtain against a debtor, allowing
the creditor to "step into the shoes" of the debtor. In
other words, if the debtor is entitled to distributions
from the FLP or LLC, the creditor may legally receive
those distributions. The charging order is meant to
allow the business to continue operating without
interruption and provides a remedy for creditors to
be paid. This can also create the beginning of the
"waiting game."

3. **What are the practical effects of the waiting game
   involving a charging order with an FLP or LLC?** The
   practical effect of a charging order is that by making
   the creditor wait for its monies (i.e., wait for a distribution from the FLP or LLC to the limited partner
   of the FLP or the LLC member), the debtor may be
   able to negotiate a more favorable settlement amount
   (i.e., a reduced settlement amount instead of the full
   amount of a judgment). Realistically, the debtor may
   need to access the monies or distributions in the FLP
   or LLC. So what happens then? In that situation, according to typical charging order rules, the creditor is
   entitled to receive the monies or distribution first (up
   to the amount of the creditor's judgment amount).
   So depending upon the personal financial situation of
   the debtor, the FLP or LLC charging order protection
   can provide a short term, medium term, or long term
   solution.

4. **What are the emerging trends involving creditors'
   remedies with FLPs and LLCs?** In the past, it was
   generally accepted that the charging order was the
   exclusive remedy for a creditor when dealing with
   LLCs and FLPs. After a monetary judgment was
   obtained against a debtor, the charging order was
   normally the only collection option permitted and
   chosen by a creditor. However, creditors have in-
   creasingly attempted (with some success) to expand

the creditor remedies that they can utilize against LLCs and FLPs. The emerging trend is to permit other remedies, including the assertion of fraudulent transfers, alter-ego piercing of the business entity shield theories, various trust theories, and creditors' bills. However, the most powerful remedy is judicial foreclosure of FLP and LLC interests by creditors. If a court judicially forecloses on a physician owner's interest, the physician owner's interest is sold to raise cash for the creditor. The buyer (who is oftentimes the creditor) effectively becomes the owner, and the physician loses all rights in the entity. The bottom line regarding the emerging trends is that creditors' remedies are expanding, and foreclosure of a debtor's interest is becoming one of the accepted remedies that a creditor may pursue.

5. **What occurs in the foreclosure of a limited partnership interest or LLC membership interest?** The following is an example of what can occur on the foreclosure of a debtor's limited partnership interest or LLC membership interest. Assume that Doctor Smith contributes $500,000 to a three–member LLC that owns a commercial real estate development. A couple of years later, Doctor Smith is sued by a creditor and the creditor obtains a judgment against him for $100,000. If Doctor Smith has formed his LLC in a state where the LLC laws provide that the "sole and exclusive remedy" for a creditor is to obtain a charging order against the debtor's interest, then the creditor would have to wait for distributions, when and if they were ever made from the LLC. If the creditor could wait for the distributions and if the distributions from the LLC would total, at some point, $100,000, then the creditor's judgment would be satisfied. If the creditor wanted to satisfy the judgment earlier, he or she could negotiate with the debtor and receive a negotiated lesser amount to satisfy the judgment. This is why some legal commentators feel

that the LLC or FLP can either be a short, medium, or long term asset protection tool. It often depends on how soon the creditor wants to get paid.

Assume the same set of facts, but the debtor is in a state in which a creditor is permitted not only the right to charge a debtor's interest in the LLC, but is also permitted to foreclose the debtor's LLC interest. If the creditor chooses the remedy of foreclosing the debtor's interest, and let's say the same creditor purchases the debtor's LLC interest, the creditor would potentially be entitled to all distributions made from the LLC without regard to the amount of the judgment. This could mean that the creditor would be entitled to all profits, surplus, and equity in the partnership property of the original debtor, including the return of the debtor's original capital contribution of the $500,000.

6. **Based upon the emerging trends of expanded creditor rights, including the laws of states that permit foreclosure and other possible creditors' remedies, what other options are available for debtors regarding FLP and LLC asset protection?** The answer to this question requires you to focus on, analyze, and consider forming business entities in the states that offer the charging order as the "sole and exclusive" remedy to creditors. There are a number of states with very protective statutes in this regard and, whenever possible, clients are advised to utilize LLCs in these states.

The Typical Limitations of The Charging Order

As mentioned earlier, the charging order is a court order that instructs the FLP/LLC to pay the debtor's share of distributions to his/her creditor until the creditor's judgment is paid in full. The debtor's share of distributions is legally also considered an "assignment" (to the extent granted) of the debtor's interest. In this context, the debtor may also be referred to as an assignee. When and if a distribution is made, it is made to the creditor. More important, *everything we will describe below assumes that your FLP or LLC operating agreement is properly drafted and all formalities are followed.* With such drafting and administration, the charging order *does not*:

- Give the creditor FLP/LLC voting rights.

- Force the FLP general partner or LLC managing member to pay out any distributions to partners/ members.

While the charging order may seem like a powerful remedy, you do need to understand and consider its status and its limitations. It is a temporary interest that may have to be renewed. In addition:

1. It is only available after a successful lawsuit. The charging order is only available after the creditor has successfully sued and won a judgment. Only then can the creditor ask the court for the charging order. It must be noted that once the threat of a charging order exists, and even while a lawsuit is proceeding, FLP/LLC assets are completely untouchable by creditors and are available for you to use (so long as you avoid fraudulent transfers).

2. It does not afford voting rights—so you stay in complete control. Despite the charging order, you remain the general partner of your FLP (or managing member of the LLC). You make all decisions about whether the FLP/LLC buys assets, distributes earnings to its partners or members, shifts ownership interests, and so forth. Judgment creditors cannot vote you out because they cannot vote your shares. Thus, even after creditors have a judgment against you, you still make all decisions concerning the FLP/LLC, including whether to pay distributions to the owners.

3. It does not grant to the debtor/assignee any management rights in the FLP or LLC.

4. It does not grant to the debtor/assignee any partner or membership rights in the FLP or LLC.

5. It does not create, in favor of the debtor/assignee, any fiduciary duty in the general partner of the FLP or the manager of the LLC.

6. It does not permit a debtor/assignee to force a dissolution of the FLP or LLC.

7. The creditor may have to pay the tax bill. The real "kicker" is how the charging order may backfire on creditors for income tax purposes. Because taxes on FLP/LLC income are passed through to the parties who are entitled to the income, the FLP/LLC does not pay tax. Each partner/member is responsible for his/her share of the FLP/LLC income. This income is taxable regardless of whether the income is actually paid out.

Depending upon how aggressive the creditor is and the extent to which the creditor "charges" the interest of the debtor or the extent to which the creditor is granted a "charge" of the interest of a debtor, the creditor could be faced with a tax bill, even though no distribution was actually received. If a creditor obtains from a court a charging order for just the debtor's proportionate share of the FLP or LLC distributions (i.e., the profits), this "charging order" will probably be considered similar to a garnishment order and the debtor/owner will be stuck with any tax bill generated by the FLP or LLC distribution, even after the distributions to the creditor.

However, if a creditor with a charging order against an FLP partner or LLC member goes to the step of "foreclosing" on the charging order (i.e., the creditor in such case would be the owner of this FLP or LLC interest), the creditor's interest will then become more permanent. This could also have the effect of making the creditor potentially liable for all of the income attributable to the charged interest of the debtor. At this point, it could be argued that the creditor steps into the shoes of the debtor for income tax purposes with respect to the FLP/LLC interest—resulting in receipt of the debtor's tax bill for income taxes on the debtor's share of the FLP/LLC income (see Revenue Ruling 77-137 and Evans v. Commissioner 447 F.2nd 547 (7th Cir. 1971)). This tax liability could exist even though the creditor will likely never receive any income. Once this occurs, aggressive creditors may become even more motivated to settle—as they have swallowed the tax poison pill without even realizing it.

Case Study: William and Donna Are Protected by FLPs

Let's examine spouses William and Donna. William is an orthopaedic surgeon and Donna a teacher. After two years of employment, William's assistant, Maribel, sues William for sexual harassment and wins an award of $750,000. Once Maribel discovers, through a debtor's examination, that William and Donna's personal assets are owned by their LLCs, what can she do?

She cannot seize the vacation home or stocks owned by the LLCs. State laws prohibit that. She also has no fraudulent transfer claim because the LLCs were created in advance of her claim. She can get a charging order on William's 39% share of the LLCs, but William and Donna would still control the LLCs and they would make no distributions. Maribel would therefore not receive any distributed profits, only potentially a tax bill on stock dividends that William and Donna never distributed. This charging order will not sound too inviting to Maribel, will it?

Maribel could look only to William's assets not owned by the LLCs. Because William had an incomplete asset protection plan and kept about $75,000 of exposed equity in the primary home, William settled the judgment for just that—$75,000 cash. William and Donna's LLCs helped them avoid financial disaster and settle the claim for pennies on the dollar. Moreover, they never lost control of their assets.

You may wonder why we have such protective laws for limited partnerships and limited liability companies. The charging order law, which can be traced back to the *English Partnership Act of 1890*, is aimed at achieving a particular public policy objective: Business activities of a partnership should not be disrupted because of non-partnership related debts of the individual partners. The rationale for this objective is that if non-debtor partners and the partnership were not at fault, why should the entire partnership suffer? American law has adopted this policy for over 100 years, culminating in the charging order law of the Uniform Limited Partnership and Uniform Limited Liability Company Acts. (Note Well: The same is not true for general partnerships!)

Three Tactics for Maximizing FLP/LLC Protection

You now understand the basic strategy for using FLPs/LLCs: Personal assets are placed into an FLP/LLC to protect them from personal creditors. This is basic "outside" asset protection. You can also be protected from claims arising from assets "inside" the FLP/LLC. Beyond this, there are four basic rules:

1. **Don't put all your eggs in one basket.** Life is full of uncertainties. One never knows when a court of law is going to make a surprise departure or deviation from accepted legal norms or precedents. One never knows when an asset within a single FLP/LLC could cause a lawsuit. Because our clients understand that they cannot control court decisions or the litigious nature of society, they protect their assets by titling them in multiple FLP/LLC arrangements (among other tools discussed in this Lesson), often in states outside their home state—in states with the best LLC/FLP rules—to title their assets. Titling your assets in different legal entities makes it more difficult for creditors to come after your entire wealth because they may have to conduct more investigations, file more motions with the court, and, perhaps, even travel to different states and hire lawyers licensed to practice in each of those states. The more entities used, the more difficult it will be for your creditors to

attack your wealth and the more likely it will be that you can negotiate more favorable settlements.

2. **Segregate the dangerous eggs from the safe ones.** Separating safe assets from dangerous assets increases the "inside" asset protection for the safe assets. In other words, since no dangerous assets are within the same entity as the safe assets, a lawsuit arising from a dangerous asset will not threaten the safe assets if the safe assets are in their own LLC. As we explained at the beginning of the chapter, dangerous assets should be owned by an LLC rather than by an FLP because LLCs give better "inside" protection. The general partner of an FLP can be personally liable for acts within the FLP, but the managing member of an LLC cannot be personally liable for the acts within the LLC.

3. **If possible, use LLCs or FLPs in the most protective states.** Not all LLCs and FLPs are created equal. They vary greatly in their asset protection, estate, and tax benefits based on the experience and expertise of the attorney drafting the operating agreement and the states in which they are formed. Some states offer much more protective language in their LLC or FLP statutes than others, and it would be unwise to form an LLC with an attorney who is unfamiliar with the differences from state to state.

Some state statutes are more creditor-friendly, while others are more debtor-friendly. In addition, many states have adopted uniform language. However, each state's courts may adopt different interpretations of similar statutes. Further, over time, courts within a state may have a change of opinion. Thus, our doctor clients use legal entities domiciled in jurisdictions that offer the best laws, and they make sure that a member of their team is an asset protection expert, keeping an eye on developments in the field so that they can switch state domiciles if necessary.

The Diagnosis

Since exempt assets generally can't protect 100% of your assets, other techniques must be used to achieve optimal asset protection. FLPs and LLCs are two of the most frequently employed asset protection tools we use to manage the wealth of doctors and their families. We would be surprised if you did not use at least one as part of your new comprehensive financial plan.

Divorce Protection

Of all the risks to orthopaedic surgeons, the most common threat to financial security may be divorce. According to the United States Census Bureau's 2002 statistics, only 33% of marriages in the United States will last 25 years. *Divorce Magazine* reports that remarriages end in divorce 60% of the time. Undoubtedly an emotionally devastating experience, divorce can be a financially disastrous experience as well—and physicians are not immune from these statistics.

Divorce protection is not about hiding assets from a soon-to-be ex-spouse. Nor is it about cheating or lying to keep your wealth. Rather, it involves resolving issues of property ownership and distribution before things go sour. By agreeing in advance what will be yours and what will be your spouse's, you save money, time, and emotional distress in the long run. In fact, this type of asset protection planning inevitably benefits all parties—except the divorce lawyers, of course.

Divorce planning is also about shielding family assets from the potential divorces of children and grandchildren. Given the statistics enumerated above, it is almost a certainty that either a child or grandchild of yours will get divorced. Thus, for purposes of intergenerational financial planning, this is a crucial topic, unless you want to give half of your legacy to the ex-spouses of your heirs. This is a lesson wealthy families have known, and addressed, for decades. Wealthy families do not have a secret to avoiding divorce. Wealthy families do have a secret to avoiding the financial losses that can be associated with inevitable divorces. This chapter will discuss why divorce can be so financially devastating, the pros and cons of prenuptial agreements, irrevocable Trusts, and ways to protect your children from divorce.

Why Divorce Can Be a Financial Nightmare

You do not have to read newspapers to see how financially devastating a divorce can be. While high-profile divorces involving hundreds of millions of dollars illustrate the point dramatically, most of us need only look to family or friends to see how a divorce turns into financial upheaval. The prevailing attitude toward divorce can be illustrated by a scene from the movie The First Wives Club. In the film, Ivana Trump explains her theory of divorce to three ex-wives, played by Goldie Hawn, Diane Keaton, and Bette Midler. "Don't get even," she says. "Get everything!"

Combine this fight-for-everything attitude with the terrible odds of facing a divorce, and you have a very serious threat to financial security. In fact, a divorce threatens not only former spouses, but also their families, and possibly their business partners as well. To truly understand how a divorce affects the finances of the participants, you must first understand how property is divided when the marriage is dissolved.

Community Property States

Many of the country's Western states have Community Property law. Community Property law stipulates that if there is no valid pre- or post-marital agreement, the court will equally divide any property acquired during the marriage other than inheritances or gifts to one spouse. Even the appreciation of one spouse's separate property can be divided if the other spouse expended effort on that property during the marriage, and the property actually appreciated concurrent or subsequent to the effort so expended. Based on these facts, it is obvious that how the asset is titled is not the controlling factor. Instead, *when* the asset was acquired and *how* it was treated are far more important factors in determining how the asset will be treated.

Equitable Distribution States

Non-community property states are called "equitable distribution" states, because courts in these states have total discretion to divide the property "equitably" or fairly. The court will normally consider a number of factors in deciding what is equitable, including the length of the marriage, the age and conduct of the parties, and the present earnings and future earning potential of each former spouse. The danger of equitable divorces is that courts often distribute both non-marital assets (those acquired before the marriage) as well as marital assets (those acquired during marriage), in order to create a fair arrangement. In this way, courts often split up property in ways that the ex-spouses never wanted or expected.

Can A "Pre-Nup" Protect You?

A premarital agreement (a.k.a. prenuptial agreement, premarital contract, ante-nuptial agreement, etc.) is the foundation of any protection against a divorce. The premarital agreement is a written contract between the spouses. It specifies the division of property and income upon divorce, including disposition of specific personal property, such as family heirlooms. It also states the responsibilities of each party with regard to their children after divorce. Finally, these agreements lay out the respective responsibilities during marriage, such as the financial support each spouse can expect or which religion will be used to raise future children. The agreement cannot limit child support because the right to child support lies with the child and not the parent.

Because a premarital agreement is a contract, the parties can customize the agreement to their particular situation and mutually determine what property is to remain the separate property of either spouse. In short, a premarital agreement should not be looked upon as an all or nothing planning strategy. For example, the doctor spouse may determine that all he wants to have his prenuptial agreement cover is his medical practice and the real estate that he owns which is associated with the medical practice. In this instance all other property would potentially be considered marital property.

Irrevocable Spendthrift Trusts: Ideal Tools to Keep Assets "In the Family"

As mentioned earlier, Irrevocable Trusts are very effective asset protection tools because the grantor no longer own the assets owned by the Trust. In other words, the grantor has transferred the property with no strings attached. Because the grantor neither owns nor controls the property, future creditors, including an ex-spouse, cannot claim the property. Moreover, the grantor can make children, grandchildren, and even future great-grandchildren beneficiaries of an Irrevocable Trust. However, even though they can benefit from Trust assets, the Trust can be drafted so that their creditors, including divorcing ex-spouses, cannot get to Trust assets.

Nonetheless, using an Irrevocable Trust should not be taken lightly. Giving away assets forever with no strings attached can prove to have serious consequences when protecting against divorce, lawsuit, or other threats. When would such a strategy make sense? It would make sense in circumstances where you would have inevitably given away the assets to certain beneficiaries anyway. For example, the Trust might be used for assets that (1) you will leave to your children or grandchildren when you die, and (2) you do not need for your financial security. For a more detailed example, consider Irving's case study.

Case Study: Irving's Trust Protects His Summer Home

Irving, a sports medicine physician, bought a summer home by a lake. He and his first wife had three small children. Unfortunately, they divorced about six years into their marriage. In the settlement, he received the summer home.

Fifteen years later, Irving was ready to marry again, now in Santa Fe, New Mexico (a community property state). Both he and his prospective spouse had been married previously and understood divorce. Irving considered a premarital agreement to keep the summer home as his separate property. He had planned to give it to his three children, but wondered whether working on the home would jeopardize this plan if he later divorced.

After speaking with Irving, we noted three important points:

1. Irving's handiwork on the home might make it marital property;
2. Irving's children and their families used the home throughout the year; and
3. Irving had a lawsuit from a failed real estate venture.

Given these points, it was clear that the best strategy for Irving was to have an Irrevocable Trust own the summer home, which would give beneficial interests of the home to all three children equally (which already occurred).

By using an Irrevocable Trust to own the summer home, Irving protected the home against possible future divorce and also shielded it from other creditors and lawsuits. By including spendthrift provisions, Irving protected the home from his children's creditors, as well. This will insure that the summer house stays in the family for generations.

Protect Your Children From Divorce

When your children or grandchildren come to you, giddy with exciting news about their recent engagements, the last thing they want to hear you ask is, "Are you going to sign a pre-nuptial agreement?" In fact, if you weren't paying for the wedding, you might lose your invitation for making such a statement.

As you learned earlier, the secret to protecting assets from divorce is keeping them as "separate property" and not commingling them with community or marital property. You can't trust your children to do this, so you are going to do it for them—without requiring the consent of your child or the future (or existing) spouse.

By leaving assets to your children's Irrevocable Trusts, with the appropriate spendthrift provisions, rather than to them personally, you can achieve this goal. They can even act as trustee of the trust you create for them. Of course, if the children take money out of the Trust and use it to buy a home or other property, that property will be subject to the rules of their state. To illustrate this point, let's look at the example of Rob and Janelle.

Case Study: Janelle's Divorce and Her Inheritance

Rob and Janelle were college sweethearts who got married right after graduation. Within a few years, their romance quickly turned sour and Rob could no longer handle the physical and emotional abuse. However, during their three-year marriage, Janelle received a sizeable inheritance and used it to pay off the couple's home. When they filed for divorce, Rob's attorney successfully argued that his time and labor on the house, and the fact that he lived in it except when Janelle occasionally kicked him out and he had to stay at his mother's, made half of the equity in the home (or $100,000) Rob's fair share. Though Rob and all of his friends will argue the $100,000 was a small consolation for what he endured, Janelle's grandparents certainly didn't intend for Rob to receive their inheritance.

What could Janelle have done differently to ensure that she protected her assets? Her grandparents could have left her the inheritance through an Irrevocable Trust that only allowed her to take out so much money per year. In that case, she would have used the interest from the inheritance to pay the mortgage down each month. If she had done so, the corpus of the inheritance would have remained separate property and would not have been part of the divorce settlement. In the short three years of their marriage, they would have had next to no equity in their home and Rob would have left the divorce with what he brought into the marriage and his wounded pride—but none of Janelle's grandparents' life savings. It is left to the reader to determine what is equitable; we aren't marriage counselors. We are only trying to help you reach your desired objectives.

In a nutshell, a little proactive financial planning can go a long way toward making sure that a divorce doesn't completely disrupt a family's financial situation.

Divorce Protection for Inherited Assets

Inherited assets that are segregated and not comingled with marital assets are protected from divorce in most states. If you have the potential to receive a consequential inheritance from your parents—and especially if you are concerned about the durability of your marriage—you should want to receive your inheritance in trust.

It is often wise for our physician clients to spend time and energy (and maybe even money) on their parents' estate and financial planning to make certain they receive their inheritances in a protected form. Inheritances received in properly designed and drafted lifetime irrevocable inheritance trusts—even if the doctor becomes the trustee of that inheritance trust upon his or her parents' deaths—are protected from divorce and can be exempt from the claims of personal and professional lawsuit creditors.

In other words, if the relationship with your parents permits, you can ask them to do for you that which you are doing for your own children.

The Diagnosis

Divorce will be a reality for many physicians, and orthopaedic surgeons are not immune to the risk. The most effective planning is done before the marriage, but there are some tactics that can be put into place even later. Contact us if this is a concern of yours.

Protecting Your Ability to Practice

As Peter remarked in his thoughts on the subject, protecting your ability to practice surgery is likely the most important risk to plan against. He may be right! According to marketing materials of more than one life insurance company:

"Probability of at least one long-term disability
(90 days or longer) occurring before age 65 is:
50% for someone age 25; 45% for someone age 35;
38% for someone age 45; and 26% for someone age 55."

Inadequate disability income insurance coverage can be more costly than death, divorce, or a lawsuit. Responsible financial planning includes *planning for the best possible future while protecting against the worst possible events*. No one ever plans on becoming disabled—though **half** of those aged 25 will have a disability of three months or longer at least once. This chapter explains not only why you need disability insurance, but also what to look for in a disability policy.

The Need for Disability Insurance

In our opinion, the disability of the orthopaedic surgeon/family breadwinner can be more financially devastating to a family than premature death. In both cases, the breadwinner will be unable to provide any income for the family; however, in the case of death, the deceased earner is no longer an expense to the family. Yet, if the breadwinner suddenly becomes severely disabled, he or she still needs to be fed, clothed, and cared for by medical professionals or family members. In many cases, the medical care alone can cost hundreds of dollars per day. Thus, with a disability, income is reduced or eliminated *and* expenses increase. This can be a devastating turn of events and can lead to creditor problems and even bankruptcy.

If you are older (near retirement) and have saved a large enough sum of money to immediately fund a comfortable retirement, then you probably don't need disability income protection. Of course, you may have some long-term care concerns, a topic which is covered in the next chapter. On the other hand, if you are under 50 years old, or if you are older than 50 and have several pre-college–age children, you should consider *the right* disability insurance a necessity. The challenge is determining what type of disability income policy is right for you.

Employer–Provided Coverage Often Inadequate

If you are an employee of a university or other large corporation, your employer may provide long-term disability coverage. The premiums are probably discounted from what you would pay for a private policy. We advise you take a good look at what the employer-offered policy covers, and buy a private policy if you and the insurance professional on your advisory team decide you need it. For many people, this makes a lot of sense, because employer-provided group policies are often inadequate. They may limit either the term of the coverage or the amount of benefits paid. For instance, benefits may last only a few years, or benefit payments may represent only a small part of your annual compensation. Since this is most commonly an employer-paid benefit, the money received during your disability will be taxed as income to you. For most, this arrangement would result in your taking home less than half of the original amount in your paycheck after taxes are paid!

Give Yourself a Check-Up

Most people with employer-provided disability insurance coverage will find the benefits inadequate. To help you determine where your existing coverage may be lacking, we have provided some questions for you to ask when you are giving yourself an insurance check-up. When you are ultimately working with the insurance professional on your advisory team, you should keep some of these questions in mind as well. They will help you better compare coverage options from different companies so that you can find the best policy for your specific circumstances and goals. Below is a list of some questions you should ask yourself, as well as short explanations of the appropriate answers:

- How long does the disability coverage last?

- How much is the benefit? (Some plans may cap the benefits at $5,000 per month.)

- What percentage of your income is covered? Though most group LTD plans are good for the purpose that they serve, they are only a partial cure. Because of the limitations or "cap," they have a built–in discrimination against higher income employees—like you!

- Who pays the premiums? (TIP: If you pay the premiums yourself, and not as a deductible expense through your business or practice, your benefits will be tax-free.) You may be seduced by the income tax deduction of the premiums, but the extra tax burden today is much easier to swallow than the tax burden will be if you suffer a disability and have a significantly reduced income and increased expenses. When you and your family need the money the most, you will have more.

- Is the policy portable, or convertible, to an individual policy if you leave the group? If so, do you maintain your reduced group rate?

- If your business distributes all earnings from the corporation at year-end in the way of bonuses to all owners/partners (typical of C-corps as a way to avoid double taxation), you should see whether these amounts are covered by the group policy. If not, and if bonuses or commissions make up a substantial part of your income (which we have seen to be the case with many people), you'll probably need supplemental coverage.

- What is the definition of disability in the group policy? Own-occupation, any occupation, or income-replacement? (Please see the discussion of these three terms below.)

- Are your overhead expenses covered if you are disabled? If you can't perform your duties at work, will the business keep paying you? If you can't generate income for the business, many of your expenses will keep on piling up, won't they? For professionals, a business overhead expense policy also covers hiring an outside professional to replace the insured during disability for up to two years.

Getting the Best Insurance Coverage for the Money

Now that you have given yourself a checkup and realize that you may need a new or supplemental insurance policy, you need to know what to look for in order to get the best coverage available at a reasonable rate. The following questions are important for you to ask when considering a disability policy.

What is the benefit amount? Most policies are capped at a benefit amount that equals 60% of income. Some states and insurance companies have monthly maximums as well. You have to ask yourself how much money your family would need if you were to become disabled. Generally, you want to find companies that offer at least 60% of pre-disability after-tax income with maximums of at least $7,500 or $10,000 monthly. There are additional monthly benefits of $5,000 to $25,000 per month available through more specialized channels for those high earners who want more monthly income than the traditional limits.

What is the waiting period? This is the period of time that you must be disabled before the insurance company will pay you disability benefits. The longer the waiting period before benefits kick in, the less your premium will be. Essentially, the waiting period serves as a deductible relative to time—you cover your expenses for the waiting period, then the insurance company steps in from that point forward. This is not unlike the deductible you have on your car, except that auto insurance deductibles are in the form of amounts paid ($100, $250, $500, etc.), not relative to a period of time. If you have adequate sick leave, short-term disability, and an emergency fund, and can support a longer waiting period, choose a policy with a longer waiting period to save money. Though waiting periods can last as long as 730 days, a 90-day waiting period may give you the best coverage for your money.

How long will coverage last? It's a good idea to get a benefit period of coverage that lasts until age 65, at which point Social Security payments will begin. Be aware that many policies cover you for only two to five years. Unless you are 62 to 65 years old, this would be an inadequate period, because most people want coverage that pays them until age 65. Unless you are so young that you haven't yet had time to qualify for Social Security, a policy that provides lifetime benefits, at costly premiums, is generally not worth the added expense.

What is the definition of disability in your policy? Definitions vary from insurance company to insurance company, and even from policy to policy within the same company. The definition of disability used for a particular policy is of the utmost importance. The main categories are Own-occupation, Any-occupation, and Loss of Income. The Own-occupation policies, which pay a benefit if you can't continue in your own occupation (even if you can and do work in another occupation after the disability), are the most comprehensive and, of course, the most expensive. Two important elements to look for in an Own-occupation policy are:

1. Are you forced to go back to work in another occupation?

2. Will you receive a partial benefit if you go back to work slowly after the disability and still make less than you did before the disability?

Does the policy offer partial benefits? If you are able to work only part-time instead of your previous full-time hours, will you receive benefits? Unless your policy states that you are entitled to partial benefits, you won't receive anything unless you are totally unable to work. Also, are Extended Partial Benefits paid if you go back to work and suffer a reduction in income because you cannot keep up the same rigorous schedule you had before you became disabled? For example, this would be an important benefit for anesthesiologists, as they often work excessive hours in their younger years and most likely will work less after any disability.

Important Note: Partial benefits may be added on as a rider in some policies and should be seriously considered, as only 3% of all disabilities are total disabilities. Some policies even have a recovery benefit: In the event that a business has lost clients during the disability due to the insured not being able to service them and the insured has suffered a loss of income because of this, there may be a benefit payable. The insured does not have to be disabled at all; there can be just loss of income due to disability-related attrition.

Is business overhead expense (BOE) covered? When you go out on your own, the last thing you think about is how you *won't* be able to pay your bills. Whether you have $10,000 or $20,000 of monthly disability benefit, you likely don't have enough to cover your lost income PLUS the costs of running the business. Though most companies have limited how much an individual can get in monthly benefit (often 60% of after-tax monthly income, capped at $10,000 per month), many carriers still offer up to $25,000 or more per month to cover business overhead expense. Many business owners who contact us have failed to implement this important defensive policy.

Is it non-cancelable or guaranteed renewable? The difference between these two terms—non-cancelable and guaranteed renewable—is very important. If a policy is "non-cancelable," you will pay a fixed premium throughout the contract term. Your premium will not go up for the term of the contract. If it is "guaranteed renewable," it means you cannot be cancelled, but your premiums could go up. As long as non-cancelable is in the description of the policy, you are in good shape.

How financially stable is the insurance company? Before buying a policy, check the financial soundness of your insurer. If your insurer goes bankrupt, you may have to shop for a policy later in life, when premiums are more expensive. Standard & Poor's top rating for financial stability is AAA. A.M. Best Co. uses A++ as its top rating for financial strength. Duff and Phelps rates companies on their ability to pay claims and uses AAA as its highest rating. Moody's uses Aa1 to rate excellent companies. There are no guarantees in life, but buying a policy from a highly rated company is the safest bet you can make, and we would not recommend gambling on your disability insurance to save a few dollars.

Other issues to consider when determining if you are getting the best disability insurance coverage for your money so that you can avoid financial disasters caused by the disability of the breadwinner in your family include:

- Increased Coverage
- Cost-of-Living Increases
- Waiver-of-Premium
- Return-of-Premium Waiver
- Unisex Pricing
- HIV Rider

- Multi-Life Pricing Discounts
- Protection of Future Pension Contributions

Disability of A Business/Practice Partner

The disability of a business partner has the potential to be just as financially crippling as the disability of the family breadwinner. There is a strong financial tie between business partners. The financial dependence between business partners can be even stronger than that between spouses. When a partner becomes disabled, the business will undoubtedly lose significant revenue while possibly facing increased costs in an attempt to replace the disabled partner. This will put a significant strain on the remaining partner, who now needs to run the business without the help of the deceased partner and replace the income of the disabled partner. Absent a buy-sell agreement tied to disability income insurance with a lump sum payout to generate funds to buy out the disabled partner and have sufficient funds to pay for a replacement physician, the end result could be financial devastation for the remaining partner and the business.

The Diagnosis

The likelihood of a disability may be greater than the probabilities of a premature death, a successful lawsuit, and a bankruptcy combined. As an orthopaedic surgeon, you see patients who are hurt and can't go back to work all the time. Most surgeons know this is a risk, but fail to adequately address it in their own planning. A disability income insurance policy is the best way to protect your future income. We cannot overstate the importance of having a comprehensive disability policy as part of any personal financial plan and a policy as a funding mechanism for a buy-sell agreement in the case of the disability of a business partner.

What I Have Learned from a Private Practice Structure

From Peter J. Millett, MD, MSc

As someone who has spent time practicing at an academic institution and in private practice, I can see the benefits of both.

In the academic setting, advantages include a level of academic stimulation, prestige, teaching, opportunities to work with experts within and across different specialties, and additional opportunities for specialized research.

Additionally, most academic positions are employment relationships, with the school as the employer. As an employee of an educational institution, you generally do not have to worry about the business side of things. All you have to concern yourself with is your work. I know some colleagues see this as a positive. They can focus on the practice of medicine, their research, or teaching. These positive attributes, however, come at a cost—typically, a lower salary and more bureaucracy. There are also some hybrid–type academic practices where the group is run privately but organizes the academic aspects for the medical center with teaching and research.

As for private practice, the surgeons must assume more of a direct role in running the business. There are solo practices, small groups, and large group private practices. There are also single specialty and multi-specialty groups. Each of these structures has unique benefits and limitations.

An aspect of personal enjoyment I derive from private practice is engaging in the challenges of running a business while simultaneously trying to provide the optimal experience for our group's patients. Also, depending on the size and management structure of your practice, you get the added benefit of being more entrepreneurial with the business. I've also found that there is less bureaucracy in private practice.

However, in private practice, you do have many business issues to consider. Daily operations may include managing partnership agreements, reviewing ancillary revenue opportunities with surgery centers, MRIs, physical therapy units, and durable medical equipment that requires oversight and management. There may also be opportunities to get involved with real estate—for example, by owning your building and leasing out office space.

If you determine private practice is the avenue for you, you will also have to decide whether you want to be part of a small or large group. You will have to educate yourself on billing and coding issues, and you will certainly have to understand how taxes will affect your operation.

Small Groups vs. Large Groups

I have seen the advent of consolidation in medicine over the past few years and the emergence of larger and larger groups. If you take into account the economy of scale—certainly larger groups have more leverage with payors or contract facilities, image facilities, surgery centers, etc.—I think the challenge for those bigger groups is to have a strong management structure that keeps an entrepreneurial vision and tries to maximize the economics for the physicians in the group while also keeping it an enjoyable place to work. Otherwise, you could end up having the worst aspects of a large academic institution (bureaucracy, no entrepreneurial aspect, lower compensation) without any of the benefits (teaching, research etc.).

Smaller groups can be more flexible—where it is easy to make quick decisions and implement new ideas. However, they will lack the buying power of the large groups and they will likely endure all the issues small businesses everywhere face. Small groups rarely have the same level of stability as larger groups.

In my opinion, many of the people I know that have gone into orthopaedics or sports medicine are type A personalities. They are executives. They are people used to making decisions and taking on projects and responsibility. These people tend to take on more and more, engaging in larger-scale operations. They may start as a small group and end up as a large operation.

I have heard from my colleagues in larger groups that there can be a level of frustration with the lack of autonomy and control they had in a smaller environment. Some of this may be driven by geography—with smaller groups working in rural areas or small towns, and larger groups operating in large metro areas. The typical considerations of where you end up include the pay, the location, the type of practice, and the future opportunities that may exist. In any event, you will again have to assess your strengths and personality traits to determine where you will be most satisfied in your professional life.

Billing and Coding

It is really important to be knowledgeable about proper coding. It is crucial to become educated in this area, because coding drives revenues and incorrect coding can lead to liability risk. With decreases in reimbursements, it is important to obtain revenue for the work that you have done. You must focus on maintaining revenue by coding and billing appropriately.

If you are the "captain of the ship," you will be ultimately responsible for incorrect billing, so you cannot just outsource it or assign it to an employee and wash your hands of it. You must have an auditing process to ensure that billing and coding are handled properly and in compliance with the ever-changing guidelines. Continuing education on the subject, along with internal audits and reviews, will mitigate the risks and ensure that you are paid appropriately.

Taxes

In a private practice, there are additional tax strategies that can be implemented and legitimate business expenses that can be paid for with pre-tax—as opposed to after–tax—dollars. Since many of us now reside in a 50% tax bracket, it is important to consider the tax consequences of many of our financial decisions. For example, in a typical private practice it could be anything from CME–related expenses, to a building we own, to utilizing captive insurance companies for the practice.

Also, a key area to consider is how you will use benefit plans. In academic medicine or in a large practice, you may be limited to a 403(b) plan or a 401(k) plan. However, in a private practice, there may be options to save for retirement through additional retirement plans and non-qualified plans.

Final Thought

Certainly the challenges of running a business versus being a paid employee are part of an equation all physicians must use to determine where they will be most satisfied in their professional life. Some physicians enjoy the business activity and experience. Others find their satisfaction is simply practicing medicine. You must assess your personality and find the right type of environment so you can reach your highest potential and enjoy what you do.

Many of us think that our advisors, attorneys, practice management advisors, CPAs, or even CEO of the practice all give the same advice or use the same protocols. I have found in my career and by listening to my friends and colleagues that the reality is quite the opposite. Not all of us are getting the same level of advice when it comes to tax planning, or corporate structure, or benefit plans, or even practice buy-ins or exit strategies. I think the onus is on us to press our advisors for the best practices and best ideas that are out there, so we can maximize our practices from a business and economic point of view. If your advisor is not up to the challenge, you must find an advisor who is. It is your practice. It is your business. Find the people who will help you get the most out of it.

Run Your Practice as a Tax-Efficient Asset-Protected Business

David Mandell, JD, MBA, Jason O'Dell, MS, CWM,
Carole Foos, CPA and Cheyenne Brinson, CPA, MBA

TRIAGE SUMMARY: You must act as the CEO of your own practice and career, and go beyond "seeing more patients" as a primary strategy. Learn how to use leverage—especially of your advisors and assets—and take advantage of the opportunities around you.

S Corporation, C Corporation, Or Both?

If you want to explore ways to reduce taxes *and* would like to see how you can do this without having to change any of your insurance provider or Medicare provider numbers, understanding this chapter is crucial. Choosing the form and structure of one's medical practice is an important decision. Most advisors to medical practices believe that the avoidance of potential double taxation makes the S Corporation the logical choice. This conventional wisdom overlooks the potential benefits a C Corporation can offer.

NOTE: We are not discussing partnerships, proprietorships, or disregarded entity LLCs here, even though we know that some of you may be practicing in these types of entities. Each of these structures has significant tax or asset protection drawbacks. If you are utilizing one of them in your practice, be sure to contact us to discuss further.

The Tax Basics of Corporations

In the last chapter we learned that there is no reason to practice as a sole proprietorship or general partnership. This results in unnecessary lawsuit risk, in addition to the inability to take advantage of many valuable tax-deductible business expenses.

In our analysis, we need to compare and contrast C Corporations and S Corporations (recognize that PLLCs and PAs may also be taxed as an S or C corporation). All businesses that incorporate are automatically C Corporations, absent an election to become an S Corporation. Both S and C Corporations have their own tax ID numbers and are required to file tax returns with the federal and appropriate state and city tax agencies. Both entities have shareholders. Both entities can be created in any state in the country.

When a C Corporation profits, it pays tax at the corporate level. Profit is excess of income over expenses. Compensation paid to physicians, as long as it is reasonable, is deductible by the corporation. The salary received by the owner is taxable to the owner as wages. After the C Corporation pays taxes, distributions of earnings already taxed at the corporate level can be paid to the physician-owners in the form of dividends. These would generally be taxed to the physician-owners as qualified dividends, thus leading to the double taxation of such earnings. As you will see below, this drawback can be easily overcome.

An S Corporation is also a separate entity that must file its own tax return. However, the S Corporation is often referred to as a "pass through" entity. Rather than paying tax at the corporate level, all income and deductions pass through to the shareholders and the shareholders must pay tax on any S Corp income at their individual rates. Whether the income of an S Corp is paid to the physician-owners as salary or as a distribution will not impact the federal or state income tax rates that will be applied to that income for the physician. Physician salaries are subject to FICA and other employment-based taxes, whereas distributions are not.

Double Taxation—Much Ado About Nothing

Mistakenly, most physicians think of S and C Corporations as having exactly the same benefits. Since the C Corporation has a potential double taxation, most doctors and their advisors elect to form an S Corporation to avoid one more potential problem.

First, the double taxation problem can be easily avoided by reducing practice profits to zero, or close to zero, at the end of the year. This is done by thousands of medical practice C Corporations that exist today. In fact, we have seen that disproportionately more orthopaedic practices nationwide are taxed as C Corporations, compared to other specialties (unfortunately, most of these practices fail to utilize all of the potential benefits of a C Corporation structure).

Second, after you review the next section, you will see that the increased benefits C Corporations offer medical practices, including the cost (in time, not money) of using and zeroing out a C Corporation, may outweigh the benefits of an S Corporation.

Additional Deductible Benefits of a C Corporation

Contrary to much conventional wisdom, a C Corporation can be the right choice for many small entities because of the deductions it allows. The corporate deduction for fringe benefits paid to employees is generally limited for shareholders owning more than 2% of an S Corporation. However, a C Corporation enjoys a full deduction for the cost of employees' (including owner employees') health insurance, group term life insurance of up to $50,000 per employee, and even long term care premiums, without regard to age-based limitations. The C Corporation can also deduct the costs of a medical reimbursement plan. If the practice owner has a small C Corporation and a lot of medical expenses that aren't covered by insurance, the C Corporation can establish a plan that results in all of those expenses being tax deductible. Fringe benefits such as employer-provided vehicles and public transportation passes are also deductible.

In contrast, health insurance paid by an S Corporation for a more than 2% shareholder is not deductible by the corporation. The shareholder must generally take a self-employed health insurance deduction on his/her personal return and follow specific IRS procedures in order to get the same deduction there. There is a possibility that the doctor's tax return will not follow these procedures precisely. In fact, we have seen many physicians' tax returns that do not reflect the proper steps here and the doctor then risks losing their deductions in an audit. For more information on this tax trap, please contact us.

Digging Deeper on the Potential Benefits of a C Corporation (over an S)

Before some of the authors were educated on the potential benefits allowed for C corporations, we too often advised doctors to use S Corporations. However, when we realized that the potential tax benefits to many doctors can be hundreds of thousands of dollars over a career by using a C Corporation rather than an S, we changed our minds.

The two most financially significant benefits allowed by law for C corporations are the following:

1. **Only C Corporations Can Offer a Particular Fringe Benefit Plan to Owners of a Practice**
   As you will read in the next chapter, particular fringe benefit plans that often make sense for medical practices are only available to owners of C Corporations. These plans can be utilized *in addition* to qualified plans like pensions, profit-sharing plans/401(k)s or IRAs. The specifics of this plan are described in more detail in the next chapter.

2. **Only C Corporations Can Offer Doctors Full Deductibility for Long-Term Care Insurance**
   Long-term care insurance—coverage vital to preventing your family's forced spend down and loss of assets—can be deductible to a corporation. However, it is not deductible for an S corporation as to the 2%+ owners. This means that for 99% of medical practices operating as S Corporations, the insurance would not be deductible. Using the C Corporation, however, such policies would be 100% deductible. As the total premiums on this type of insurance can be over $100,000 over ten years, the total tax saving could be $40,000 or more per doctor—typically, well worth the time of creating year-end bonuses to avoid double taxation.

Changing from an S to a C Corporation

If you are already operating as an S Corporation and are interested in converting to a C, the good news is that it is extremely easy. A simple revocation of the S election can be made instantly for an S Corporation. This can be done until March 15th for that calendar year and any time for the next calendar year.

Get the Best of Both Worlds—
Why Not Use Both an S and a C?

If you are already using an S Corporation, you could consider what many practices have done—for this, and general asset protection reasons—that is, to create a second entity as a non-medical management company.

In fact, many practices can take advantage of both the C Corporation and the S Corporation by setting up two distinct entities to operate different aspects of their practice. Perhaps the S Corporation will be used for the operating side of the practice (professional practice of medicine) while the C Corporation will be used for management functions (billing and administration). In this way, the practice as a whole can take advantage of both the tax deductions and benefits afforded a C Corporation and the "flow through" advantages of an S Corporation. See the diagram on the next page. This may also provide some additional asset protection. As long as all formalities of incorporation are followed, as well as compliance with rules for employee participation in all benefit plans, medical practices can benefit from this dual corporate structure. Although perfectly legal if set up and operated correctly, it is recommended that accurate records be kept detailing the income and expenses recorded in each entity, and special attention be paid to transactions between the two entities. Because there is the potential to shift income from a higher individual bracket to a lower corporate bracket (or vice versa), the Internal Revenue Service will look for this in the event of an examination.

The Diagnosis

In this chapter, we pointed out that many of you may be using a sub-optimal tax treatment for your practice. If wealth creation and asset protection are priorities in the practice, a C Corporation should be strongly considered, and the special benefits that C Corporations allow should be closely examined. For doctors using S Corporations, it is easy to convert to a C Corporation, and to use a two-entity structure as well.

Medical Practice: Multiple Entities

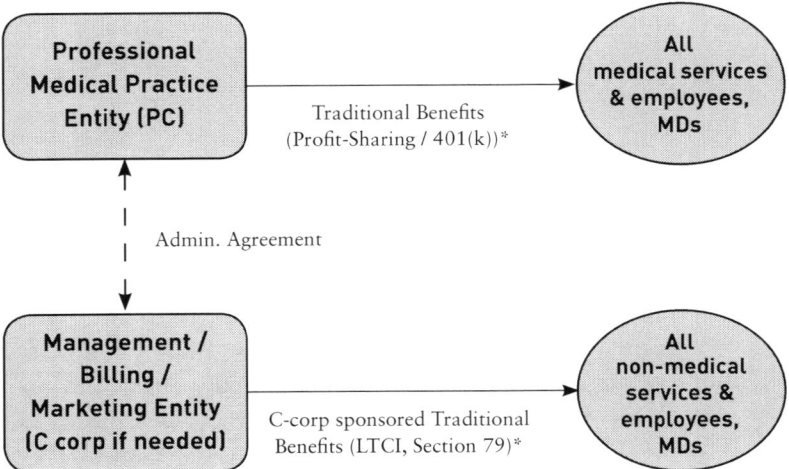

* *Affiliated Service Rules Apply*

Using Qualified, Non-Qualified, and Fringe Hybrid Plans

This chapter discusses two topics which are related and can contribute to the practice's financial benefits to the physician-owners. However, the chapter is unique in that almost every orthopaedic surgeon reading this takes advantage of the first option—qualified plans—while almost none utilize non-qualified or fringe hybrid plans. We will discuss both the common qualified retirement plans and the less common plans here, so that you can be aware of options available to you and, hopefully, get more out of your hard work, build greater wealth, and enjoy the fruits of your labor.

Qualified Retirement Plans

A qualified retirement plan is a retirement plan that complies with certain Department of Labor and Internal Revenue Service rules. You might know such plans by their specific type, including pension plans, profit sharing plans, money purchase plans, 401(k) s, or 403(b)s. Properly structured plans offer a variety of real economic benefits, such as:

- The ability to fully deduct contributions to these plans.

- Funds within these plans grow tax-deferred.

- Funds within these plans are protected from creditors.

In fact, these benefits are likely the reasons why most medical practices sponsor such plans.

For this chapter, we will include IRAs as qualified plans even though, technically, they are not. We are doing this because IRAs have essentially the same tax rules as qualified plans and have the same attractions for doctors who can use them.

Qualified plans (not IRAs), must be offered to all qualified employees (within certain restrictions). For a surgeon as owner, there may be some economic costs to having a plan that you must offer to, and contribute to, for everyone at the office or at related businesses. With these mixed benefits and drawbacks, it is surprising how many physicians (nearly 100%) use qualified plans and ignore their cousins, non-qualified plans, or fringe benefit plans. Review the following chart so you can better understand the pros and cons of qualified plans.

Benefits & Drawbacks of Qualified Plans

Benefits	Drawbacks
Tax deductible contributions	You must contribute to plan for all eligible employees
Highest level of asset protection (+5)	All withdrawals subject to ordinary income tax rates
Tax-deferred growth	Penalties for access prior to age 59½
	Must take minimum distributions at age 70½
	You are betting that future income tax rates are the same or lower
	May be taxed at 72% or more at death

Your Qualified Plan Bet on Future Tax Rates

In our other books for physicians, we cover most of the benefits and drawbacks of qualified plans in more detail. Here, we want to make sure you understand the bet you are making on future tax rates when you rely heavily on qualified plans for your retirement. Since all amounts that come out of qualified plans (and SEP and roll-over IRAs, of course) are 100% income taxable, there is no way to know how good (or bad) a financial deal such a plan could be for you until you know the tax rates when you withdraw funds.

In other words, if you contribute funds to a qualified plan today (when the top federal income tax rate is 39.6%) and withdraw funds when income tax rates are at the same or a lower level, the deduction today and tax-free growth over time is likely a pretty good deal for you. However, if you withdraw funds from your plan and the top federal tax rates are 40%-50% or higher, then the qualified plan/IRA may be a bad deal for you.

> [**Clarification Point**: Some folks may argue that, in retirement, you are likely to have less income and thus the plan distributions will be taxed at lower rates. While this may be likely for 95% of taxpayers, most of our orthopaedic surgeon clients will build enough wealth in retirement and non-retirement assets to be in the top marginal tax rates in retirement. The second highest marginal income tax rate of 35% (4.6% less than the highest rate) goes into effect when a married couple has TAXABLE income of $398,351 in 2013. Do you think that your taxable income will be less than $398,351 when you add in retirement distributions, Social Security, rental income, and any investment gains from non-pension assets? In many cases, doctors are going to retire only when their retirement assets will generate incomes equal to their last year's salary. For most of our clients, this is the retirement game plan—retire only when they can maintain the lifestyle to which they have become accustomed.]

With this is mind, review the history of US income tax rates in the chart below. Putting aside politics, you must understand that it is certainly a possibility that tax rates can return to the levels they were for most of the 20th century. If they do, qualified plans utilized today by most orthopaedic surgeons may turn out to be losing bets in the long run. Since we cannot know what future tax rates will be, we need to at least acknowledge the bet we are making and ask how we can reduce our risk and perhaps hedge against such a losing bet.

Federal Income Tax Rates

Year	Top Marginal Federal Income Tax Rate
1920*	73.0%
1930*	25.0%
1940*	81.0%
1950*	91.0%
1960*	91.0%
1970*	71.0%
1980*	70.0%
1990*	28.0%
2000*	39.6%
2010	35.0%
2013	39.6%

Source: Citizens for Tax Justice, May 2004.

A New Concept for Investing— Tax Treatment Diversification

Does the fact that our qualified plans today may turn out to be losing bets mean that we should abandon them? In most cases, the answer is "No." These plans generally have the strongest asset protection available and provide significant incentives for employees. We would strongly recommend, however, that EVERY orthopaedic surgeon make investments that offer a hedge against potential tax rate increases.

The concept here is that you should have various buckets in which to grow wealth—and each bucket should be subject to a different tax treatment. Consider it a second, but equally important, diversification technique for your wealth—along with investment class diversification.

We spread our investments across different classes of assets so that, in the event something bad happens impacting one industry or investment type, the total portfolio is not affected. With tax treatment diversification, a similar theory applies. If you have some investments that may be taxed as ordinary income, some that may be taxed at capital gains or dividend tax rates, and some assets that may not be taxable at all, you have flexibility. When ordinary income tax rates are very high, you may choose to spend assets that are taxed at low capital gains tax rates or not taxed at all. When rates are low, you may choose to pay those taxes now.

For example, some real estate investors in the last few years have NOT made 1031 exchanges. They volunteered to pay the 15% federal capital gains taxes before they were raised in 2013. Others deferred the tax and will now pay 23.8% (federal and Affordable Care Act tax—state and local are in addition) when they sell. The goal is to have flexibility so you are never at the mercy of one legislative change.

How to Hedge Your Qualified Plan Bet with Tax Treatment Diversification

Above, we have recognized that, if history is any indication of the future, federal income tax rates may rise even higher than they are today, perhaps significantly. We also understand that our qualified plans are, in fact, a bet that future tax rates will stay close to the rates today or will decrease in the future. Because such a bet is risky at best, we would all like to find a way to hedge against it. We *can* hedge against federal tax increases, using tax treatment diversification. Such diversification can be accomplished in two ways: (1) by accumulating non-qualified plan after-tax investments, and (2) by using benefit plans that are taxed differently from traditional qualified plans. Let's examine each here:

1. Using After-Tax Investments

Most orthopaedic surgeons use this technique. It is simply investing one's after-tax savings in a liquid asset class (securities, savings, CDs, etc.) that can be accessed in retirement. Because these assets can be sold without significant income tax—stock sales will typically trigger capital gains taxes, while savings, bonds and CDs trigger income taxes on relatively small interest payments—they are much better protected against a high future income tax than qualified plan distributions that are 100% income taxable. In this way, if income tax rates are very high for a period of retirement, you could use these types of assets to live on and not significantly draw down the qualified plan assets at that time. Even more importantly, by having this asset class as part of your retirement game plan, you are not as exposed to the risk of ordinary income tax rates increasing in the future.

While this technique is certainly crucial, it still has one tax risk—that capital gains tax rates will rise significantly. In fact, while we call this technique "after tax investments," this is actually a misnomer. That is because such assets will trigger capital gains taxes when they are sold and—for certain assets, like mutual funds—capital gains taxes are levied along the way as well.

Again, study the chart below. You will see that, for the past 12 years, US federal capital gains tax rates were at their LOWEST point in the history of the tax. With the Fiscal Cliff deal of early 2013, the federal capital gains and dividend tax rate for high income taxpayers rose to 20%, plus the Affordable Care Act 3.8% tax on such gains/dividends as well.

Putting politics aside, we do not think that it is unrealistic to expect that such rates will be raised again in the future. Once again, does this mean that we should abandon this asset class? Absolutely not. However, it does make sense for most physicians to examine a third tax asset class that can eliminate the risk of future income tax rate AND future capital gains tax rate increases.

Top Federal Capital Gains Tax Rates

Year	Top Marginal Federal Income Tax Rate
1940*	30.0%
1942–1967*	25.0%
1970*	32.3%
1977*	39.9%
1980*	28.0%
1990*	28.0%
2000*	20.0%
2010	15.0%
2013	23.8%**

Source: Citizens for Tax Justice, May 2004.
**Federal capital gains tax on highest income taxpayers + Affordable Care Act tax

2. Using Non-Qualified and Fringe Hybrid Benefit Plans

Non-qualified plans are relatively unknown to physicians, despite the fact that most Fortune 1000 companies make non-qualified plans available to their executives. This type of plan could be very attractive to doctors, as employees are not required to participate AND allowable contributions for the owners and executives can be much higher than with qualified plans. Because there are numerous types of non-qualified plans—from split dollar plans to 162 Executive Bonus plans among many others—we will keep our discussion here to one type of plan that has both qualified and non-qualified traits and that can provide you with excellent tax diversification—a fringe benefit plan which we call a hybrid type of benefit plan.

This hybrid plan is a very flexible plan that has numerous benefits for a medical practice. As relevant here, the contributions are partially deductible and partially taxable at the outset—which is much better today than the "after tax investments" asset class and not as good as the qualified plan. The funds grow tax-deferred, which is the same as the qualified plan and better than the "after tax investments" class. Finally, in the future, when funds are accessed in retirement, they can be reached without tax—better than the "after-tax investments" and far superior to the qualified plan. In this way, the hybrid plan avoids the risks of future income and capital gains tax rate increases in a substantial way—and can act as an ideal hedge against future income and capital gains tax increases.

In addition to playing the role as a future tax increase hedge, this plan has the following benefits:

- These plans can be utilized *in addition* to a qualified plan such as a pension, profit-sharing plan/401(k), or IRA.

- The funds in these plans can grow in the top (+5) asset protection environment in many states and in the (+2) solid level of protection in others.

- Maximum annual contribution levels are $100,000 per physician in practices with 10 employees or fewer. In larger practices, these levels can be even higher.

- In a group practice, not every physician need contribute the same amounts—extremely beneficial for group practices with doctors who want to put away differing amounts.

- The plan funding can be flexible.

- Employee participation requires a minimal funding outlay.

- There are no minimum age requirements for withdrawing income (no early withdrawal penalties).

- The transfer of assets at the participant's death is income tax-free to heirs.

The Diagnosis

Most orthopaedic surgeons in the U.S. utilize some type of qualified retirement plan, including an IRA, as part of a benefit plan. Certainly, these plans can serve both as a protective and wealth accumulation tool. On the other hand, too few doctors use, or even investigate, non-qualified, fringe benefit, and hybrid plans. This is unfortunate given the tax bet that qualified plans require—a bet that could be a losing one in the future. We hope that you make it a priority to hedge such a bet and investigate other tax asset classes such as the plans described above.

Creating Your Practice's $1 Million Retirement Buyout

One of the most common complaints we hear from physicians in general, including orthopaedic surgeons, is that they are frustrated that their decades of hard work are not building anything of concrete financial value. In other words, these doctors are frustrated that their practice will not be worth anything when they retire. As a result, they cannot sell it and enjoy a lucrative exit from the practice of medicine the way other business owners can with their non-medical businesses. Does this sound familiar?

It is certainly true that the days of an outside practice management firm coming in and purchasing a practice for millions of dollars are long gone. On the other hand, there are a number of tactics you can employ to create a $1 million buy-out fund. We are not talking about the funded Buy-Sell arrangement that applies to unforeseen circumstances such as a disability or the premature death of a partner. The buy-out funds we will discuss here are mechanisms to exit a practice at the surgeon's chosen retirement time and take more than $1 million out at that point. Of course, this would also be in addition to whatever the surgeon has in qualified retirement plans and other personal assets.

Buyout Funding Options

As you will see below, each of these tools requires periodic funding over time. With compound growth over an entire career, a doctor can create significant retirement buy-out funds over 10, 20, or 30 years. A nice bonus is that the funds can grow on a tax-deferred or tax-free basis in most of these arrangements. With all of these tools, you have two potential ways of funding them:

A. **Solo Practice Model**

Here, the physician in question simply takes advantage of one or more of the tools below and funds them from the practice. This approach is certainly better than not funding them at all, thanks to the asset protection and potential tax benefits that many of these tools afford. These options force the doctor to build the buy-out fund with dollars that might otherwise be spent on personal consumption. Therefore, any and all of these tools can be used in the one-doctor model.

B. **Group Practice Model**

In this model, in addition to the potential tax, asset protection, and forced savings benefits, physicians enjoy another crucial benefit described earlier on in the book. They get to use other people's money (OPM) to achieve a long-term goal. OPM is involved here because each of these tools can be leveraged in a way that older doctors of the practice require the younger physicians (partners or not) to contribute into these vehicles. While the contributions go partly to their own buy-out fund, part of it could also fund the buy-out of older doctors. When these younger doctors become more senior, they too will benefit from this arrangement and the funding by younger physicians at that time. This pyramid model is common in professional firms outside medicine, such as consulting or law firms.

Buyout Funding Tools

As you will see below, all the major buyout funding tools are arrangements that we have already described earlier in this Lesson. Let's examine each of them again briefly and review how they apply to the goal of creating a buyout retirement fund.

1. **LLC Lease-Back**

   A valuable piece of equipment or the practice's office can be transferred to a limited liability company (LLC) and then leased back to the practice entity. As explained in our larger book *For Doctors Only*, this provides asset protection for the practice (*vis-à-vis* claims from the property or equipment), the property/equipment (from claims against the practice), and for the doctors (from both).

   The LLC lease–back works as a buyout funding tool through the rent paid by the practice to the LLC. Each month the practice will pay tax-deductible rent to the LLC. Proceeds remain inside the LLC, asset protected at a (+2) level, if the structure/LLC is maintained properly. They can be managed by professionals in a tax-favored way and built up over time to create a buyout fund.

   Even better, in the group practice model, the doctors gain additional shares in the LLC for each year of service. This way, the older physicians have more of an interest in the LLC accounts as they remain with the practice, and the younger doctors help fund their value (as the rent can be an expense they all share equally). When the physician retires, he or she can redeem LLC interests for cash. The cycle continues as new doctors join the practice and become young partners.

2. **Unrelated Accounts Receivable (AR) Financing**

   In the unrelated lender AR financing structure, an outside lender (typically a bank) takes the security agreement against the AR. This is typically in return for a loan to the practice. Often, the loan proceeds are invested in a creditor-protected life insurance policy or annuity as part of a deferred compensation arrangement for the doctors.

   In the solo practice structure, the opportunity for a buy-out fund comes from the deferred compensation arrangement. However, as we discuss and caution in our book *For Doctors Only: A Guide to Working Less & Building More*, because loan interest must be paid to the bank, the investments of the plan should be conservatively structured to meet the loan interest and principal obligations. Sometimes, it is difficult to generate a return that exceeds the interest costs of the loan. Taking too much risk here in an attempt to generate income to offset the loan payments is extremely unwise and can lead to further negative financial consequences. Remember, the reason you are entering into this transaction in the first place is to reduce—not increase—financial risks.

For the group practice model, there may be more of an opportunity for a buy-out fund, even if the policy is a very conservative one. This is because of the OPM factor. If younger doctors share the burden of funding the policy of older physicians, there is a greater opportunity for buy-out funds accumulating beyond the loan obligations.

3. **Related AR Financing**
   In the related lender AR financing structure, a related lender (often an irrevocable trust for the benefit of non-physician family members) makes the loan to the practice and the trust takes the security agreement against the AR. Because the trust and family members (spouse and children, typically) are being paid interest, the overall family economics are superior to the unrelated lender arrangement.

   This buyout fund arrangement generally only works with solo or two-person practices, because the lender is related to the doctor. It becomes too complex to have multiple trusts loaning funds to a practice with more than one or two surgeons. However, in the small practice scenario, this arrangement can provide solid asset protection and create beneficial buy-out funds within an LLC or exempt life policy as well.

4. **Non-Qualified/Hybrid/Fringe Benefit Plan**

   Non-qualified plans (or hybrid plans) are benefit plans not required to be offered to all practice employees. While the contributions to the plan are typically not tax deductible, the funds in the plan can grow tax-deferred.

   The non-qualified plan works as a buy-out funding tool through the contributions paid by the practice to the plan. Each month or year, the practice will make contributions to the plan for each participant. The funds can then grow in the plan tax-deferred. At retirement (no age restrictions as with qualified plans), the doctor can withdraw his or her plan funds. The tax at that time depends on the plan. In the solo practice model, the orthopaedic surgeon simply has the practice make contributions to the plan and enjoys the tax-favored build–up over time to create a buyout fund.

   Even better, in the group practice model, the surgeons can gain additional benefits by using the contributions of the practice to fund the plan based on years of service. This way, the older doctors have more of an interest in the fund as they remain with the practice. The cycle continues as new doctors join the practice and become young partners.

5. **Captive Insurance Company (CIC)**

   As explained earlier, CICs are real insurance companies that insure the medical practice for a host of risks. In many cases, a surgeon's CIC can be just as profitable over their career as the medical practice. Thus, whether the doctor owns the CIC himself (solo model) or all the physicians in the practice own it, the CIC can create an enormous potential buy-out fund when any one surgeon retires. In fact, the superior structure is one where the CIC is owned from the outset by one or more Trusts for the doctors' families, and the CIC establishes some type of benefit plan for the physicians' buy-out fund. This creates estate planning benefits as well as buy-out funding benefits.

The Diagnosis

Orthopaedic surgeons, like all doctors today, cannot simply rely on a white knight firm to come in and buy their practices for millions on the day they want to retire. On the other hand, the idea that they can't get anything for their practice misses the point entirely. Sports medicine physicians who plan for an exit can have a lucrative one—but they need to focus on the goal of creating a buy-out fund years before they retire and be diligent in their funding of one or more buy-out tools over time.

Money Saving Techniques through Practice Efficiency

Like most orthopaedic surgeons, you want to save money. Unfortunately, there likely isn't a pot of gold hiding in Exam Room One, so focusing on ways to save $1,000 here and $1,000 there is in order. When times are good, we dismiss small dollar savings. In lean economic times, it's important to examine all expenses. Small dollars add up to provide substantial savings for your practice. A $10,000 reduction in expenses equates to approximately 130 Level 3 established patient office visits (99213) at Medicare rates. How many surgical cases do you have to perform to earn $10,000?

1. <u>Malpractice</u> If you are claims free, use an EHR, and/ or attend a risk management seminar, ask about a risk rewards discount. These discounts can add up to 15%. Also, shop your broker from time to time to make sure you are being presented with the best rates and companies. In Illinois, a solo orthopaedic surgeon switched carriers and saved $9,300.

2. <u>Credit Card Processing</u> New technology allows you to process credit cards through the internet, freeing up a telephone line, an average $50/month savings. Other features include recurring billing, email receipts and the ability to take payments on your website. Also, make sure that you aren't paying too much on payment processing. TransFirst will provide you a free Payment Processing Analysis. We've helped solo

and group orthopaedic practices easily save $3,600 per year. https://transfirst.com/

3. <u>Telephone Bill</u> Besides the obvious (making certain that you are paying for the correct number of telephone lines and not ones for your old office after a move), look at the technology. Some practices are using analog phone lines and residential DSL internet. Switching to digital technology or Voice over Internet Protocol (VoIP) consolidates phone lines and gives you high speed T1 internet access for a considerable monthly savings ($200-$500/month). Another strategy is to renegotiate with your current provider or shop for comparable services.

4. <u>Energy Savings</u> Go green to save some green. Turn off lights and computers at the end of the day. Install sensor controlled light switches to automatically turn off when an exam room or office is not occupied. Use energy efficient light bulbs and LED monitors. The savings accumulate over time.

   Many states have deregulated and now offer numerous choices for electricity, saving your practice money. Visit http://www.eia.gov/cneaf/electricity/page/restructuring/restructure_elect.html for a full listing of deregulated states.

5. <u>Accounting Fees</u> A good accountant is worth his or her weight in gold, but take a hard look at the services he or she is providing to you. If you are receiving monthly compilation reports several months behind, what value are you receiving? Often times, bookkeeping services are most cost–efficient when performed in house, and then have your accountant concentrate on tax planning, tax preparation services, retirement planning, and other business planning. As David and Jason point out elsewhere in the book, forward–looking tax planning is much different than backwards–looking bookkeeping and preparation of financial statements.

The same goes for payroll processing. National payroll companies offer competitive rates to process your payroll, saving you money. If you're using Quickbooks, Intuit offers full payroll services for a low monthly fee and includes direct deposit. You enter the hours and they file the payroll tax returns for you. Also, process your payroll on a bi-weekly or semi-monthly basis, not a weekly basis. Weekly payroll costs add up over the course of the year and are an administrative burden to administer. If overtime is not an issue in your practice, a semi-monthly payroll is the most cost effective payroll cycle and it evens out cash flow as it eliminates the dreaded three–pay–period month.

6. Answering Service Technology has come a long way, and AlertMD is saving surgeons money and providing an answering service in an innovative and easy way. We've seen upwards of $100/month savings per surgeon. www.alertmd.com

7. Collection Agency These costs can easily stagger. There are agencies such as Transworld Systems, an MGMA (Medical Group Management Association) AdminiServe Partner, that offers pre-collection activities for a flat dollar amount. The key to success with these types of services is to turn over the account at 75-90 days, not 180 days. The older an account is, the less likely they will collect. http://web.transworld systems.com/bclayton/

8. Computer Support If your computer support charges continue to escalate, there may be an underlying root cause; perhaps there are needed hardware or software upgrades. Also keep in mind the staff productivity loss that occurs when the staff aren't trained and don't use the program optimally, or when the computers are down. These are hidden costs that most often go overlooked and are costly.

9. Group Purchasing Organization (GPO) Join a GPO to save money. Membership has its benefits. AAOS http://www3.aaos.org/member/prac_manag/AAOS MemberAdvantageProgram.cfm and MGMA http://www.mgma.com/adminiserve/ members can join MedAssets and enjoy discounts on medical and office supplies, services, etc.

10. Medical and Office Supplies First, take inventory of what you already have—which means having everyone empty out their desk drawers! Poor inventory controls or sloppy supply closets often lead to over-ordering. Who is in control of ordering? Who selects which supplies the practice uses, or is it a free-for-all? Determine what your top 25 medical supplies and office supplies are and then shop those supplies on an annual basis. Join a GPO to receive the best rates. Insist on MD–approved purchase orders.

11. Postage Meters Shop the costs of your postage meters. Pitney-Bowes, Neopost, and Hasler are companies many practices use. Using stamps.com to print postage and forgoing an expensive postage meter can save the practice money! And, if you do billing in-house, make certain you are using an automated service to send your statements. Your clearinghouse or practice management system often offers this service for 50–60 cents per statement. The time savings alone are well worth this small investment.

Ten thousand dollars in cost savings will likely cover the cost of your medical assistant for three to four months or pay rent (depending on your geographic region, of course). **The big money savings come with an overhaul of operational efficiency.**

Salary expense is likely your number one expense. We see orthopaedic practices freeze salaries, eliminate bonuses, lay off staff, or not fill critical positions. Often, this is to the practice's detriment because patient volumes remain the same and no process improvements have been made.

The focus in recent years for many orthopaedic practices has been on implementing an electronic health record (EHR), but yet we see billing offices struggling with the technology that has been available to them for years.

Technology in the billing office is an often overlooked area which burdens practices with lost productivity, slow reimbursement, and underpayments. Use the checklist below to determine if your billing office is using the available tools to ensure the fastest reimbursement possible.

- Electronic Funds Transfer (EFT) Instead of receiving a paper check in the mail, payments are direct deposited to the practice's bank account. There is no cost to enroll, and most major payors offer EFT. Blue Cross Blue Shield of Illinois, New Mexico, and Texas, for example, offer daily payment options when enrolling in EFT. EFT reduces the number of checks staff deposit and provides a better audit control.

- Remote Deposit Capture (RDC) EFT will significantly reduce the number of insurance checks flowing to the office; however, there remain check payments from patients. For those checks, use RDC—a scanner that converts a paper check into an ACH (Automated Clearing House) transaction and deposits it into the practice's bank account. There is a monthly fee and a per transaction fee associated with RDC, but the time savings of avoiding completing a deposit slip and physically going to the bank produce a significant ROI (return on investment) for most practices. Most banks and credit card vendors offer RDC.

- Electronic Remittance Advice (ERA) ERA is the single most effective tool in reducing time in the billing office. Rather than manually keying data from an EOB (Explanation of Benefits), an electronic file is received from the payor and auto-posted. The process is coordinated through your clearinghouse. This allows billers to focus on follow–up on unpaid claims rather than tedious data entry. ERA is also the cornerstone to other services that are now offered, which are discussed below.

- Electronic Filing of Worker's Comp Claims and Secondary Claims Another game changer in recent years is the ability to electronically file worker's compensation claims with attachments electronically, even if you do not have an EHR. This is a significant time saver from having to print the claim, attach the notes, and then mail from the office. Clearinghouses are also able to file secondary claims electronically that do not automatically cross over, as long as you have ERA. This eliminates the very laborious process of using a black marker to de-identify other patients on an EOB.

- Batch eligibility Virtually all practice management systems or clearinghouses have the capability to verify the insurance of scheduled patients; however, we find very few practices using this technology, or they only use it for select patients. Pre-register all patients and allow the system to verify insurance in advance of appointments to reduce denials for "coverage not effective at date of service." Often, information about unmet deductibles for in-network providers and co-pay amounts can be returned as well, providing valuable tools for collection at the time of service.

- Cost Estimators A growing number of payors are offering cost estimators on their websites. This is a vital tool for practices to provide an estimate to patients based on CPT code(s) during financial counseling and an aid in collecting patient responsibility prior to a non-emergency procedure.

- Underpayments How does your payment poster know that you are being paid according to contract? Too often they don't know, and practices leave money on the table. Many practice management systems allow for the payor fee schedules to be loaded into the system and on a per–transaction basis compare the payment amount to the contract amount or run exception reports. We prefer more sophisticated systems of analyzing underpayments. There are third–party applications, including some clearinghouses, that analyze underpayments and allow for you to appeal those underpayments for a reasonable cost.

The biggest mistake we see orthopaedic practices make is not utilizing the expensive practice management system (PMS) and/or electronic health record (EHR) to its fullest potential. Old paper workflows are still utilized, although the workflow could be automated, streamlining the process and saving a significant amount of time. The surgery scheduling workflow is a glaring example of lost productivity. The diagram on the following page illustrates how the surgery scheduling workflow can be automated.

The Diagnosis

Opportunities exist in most orthopaedic practices to save money. The low hanging fruit is examining common expenses for potential savings. In order to save the big money, practices must take a hard look at practice operations and identify efficiencies that can be garnered by automating workflows. The proper use of technology tools can lead to great efficiency in the reimbursement cycle and other back–office areas, significantly reducing practice overhead and leveraging the cost of expensive software the practice has already invested in.

Decision for surgery	• Surgery workflow is initiated • Physician is prompted to document "medical necessity" criteria based on surgery and payor • Physician creates an "order" for the surgery (similar to labs) and indicates planned CPT codes and Dx codes
Financial Counseling	• Surgery scheduler receives notification of surgery order in queue • Surgery scheduler meets with patient to discuss financial responsibility. Uses online tools for claims estimator and benefit calculation • Collects and posts surgery deposit
Surgery Scheduled	• Surgery booking forms are generated from EHR and auto-completed from patient chart. Any additional information is added • Surgery booking form is e-faxed directly from EHR to hospital or surgery center • Surgery is placed on computerized schedule and post-op visit scheduled (no "black" book)
Patient Communications	• Patients are e-mailed instructions and post-op instructions directly from EHR
Pre-Certification	• Pre-cert forms and/or prior-authorization letters are auto-generated from information in patient's chart in the EHR, along with any progress notes (when required)
Follow-Up	• Patients who do not schedule surgery are properly tracked and follow-up initiated • Can accurately calculate surgery acceptance and visit to surgery ratio • All notes are recorded in EHR
Surgery Performed	• Op notes received from hospital either via fax or downloaded from their portal • Op notes compared to CPT codes and Dx codes as submitted by physician for coding accuracy; any conflicts are reviewed with the physician
Submit Claim	• Surgery charges are entered and submitted for claims processing • Payor rules are followed for claims submission (i.e. unilateral versus bilateral claims)
Appeals	• Surgery scheduler reviews any denials or low reimbursement from payor. Appeals as necessary.

Physicians As Investors: The Good, The Bad, & The Ugly

From from Peter J. Millett, MD, MSc

Mistakes I Have Made

One of the biggest mistakes I have made in my financial planning is being too trustworthy of people that have come to me with investment opportunities and or alleged deals. You have to have a healthy skepticism or level of caution, especially when dealing with startups, and private investments—like real estate deals.

"A fool and his money are soon parted," and many of us are naïve when we start our practices. Many younger doctors reading this probably don't realize how many financial advisors there actually are out there. However, after you have been in practice for a while and start making a little bit of money, people will come to you with investment opportunities.

Many of these opportunities will sound very enticing, but remember that more often than not, your entire principal will be at risk. One of the mistakes I've made is being naïve and too often believing that the risky investments would actually achieve the results the promoters and company executives promised at the outset.

There are many different investment philosophies out there. We will discuss a few below. You can become involved in private equity deals, and you can look for ways to utilize leverage and generate passive income, or you can stick with basic long-term investment vehicles. Whatever you choose, you will also have to consider how to protect what you accumulate. Further, consider your actual returns versus your paper returns. Taxes, fees, and additional costs can eat into your returns; -really, all that should matter to you is what you actually get to keep. There are many new and exciting investment opportunities, but in order to really do your due diligence, it helps to have a trusted advisor who can choreograph all the moving parts and differing aspects of your plan—someone who can get your investment advisor, attorneys, and tax people on the same page.

If you are smart in your planning, tax efficient in your practice, and careful in your investments, with time you can do very well with a conservative return due to the power of compound interest. As Warren Buffett said, the secret to investing is having "good snow and a very long hill!"

Private Equity Pitfalls

Private equity pitfalls are similar to those in the startup and real estate space. If I think about all of the private equity deals I've invested in, probably some of the best ones I have made are those that have a tangible asset which can come back to you even if the business deal goes south—like income–producing real estate, or a venture in which the business is already profitable. Of course, these are also less risky deals, so the upside is also much more limited than with a true startup or a real estate deal starting with raw land.

Given my practice area, I have gotten involved in various surgery and medical device–related tech investments. Technology is generally a high risk investment category. Physicians tend to be attracted to these deals because they come to us in a very early startup phase, so there is great upside potential. Also, because we know the field, we believe we understand the product niche and think we may have some influence on the management team or have a true insight into the potential to help surgeons and assist in getting the product to the marketplace. Certainly, I think it is okay to allocate some of your money to venture capital investing in areas related to our field, but you want to make sure to realize that this is risk capital, and it should be highly offset by more traditional liquid equities like stocks, bonds, and cash, and more tangible assets like real estate.

Also, be aware that going from product concept to a successful, profitable enterprise is very challenging. I have seen many great tech ideas never see the light of day after millions were invested. Be aware that just because the company stays in business, that doesn't mean that you as an investor are getting your investment back or a profit out of the deal. That takes dividends payments, or even a "liquidity event," which is even rarer. Keep your eyes wide open when investing in these deals, and make certain that you fully understand and appreciate the risks.

Another mistake I've made when investing in private deals is not getting good documentation at the outset. If a promoter or executive tells you something about the deal, especially a material point about the company, its technology, the financial upside, etc., you want to be sure you get it in writing.

Try to further determine what will happen if the event does not go as planned. A good investor knows the downside risk up front and will figure out their exit strategy if necessary. Be sure to keep your records—ideally, in a secure place, or even better, on-line, where there is security but no risk of losing the documents. I know there are some good online vaults out there designed for this purpose.

By maintaining your documentation, if, in the future, there is a misunderstanding or even bad actors, you have clear records of what was discussed when, and what the terms of the deal were. If you are meticulous about saving communications with people, it becomes easier to resolve a dispute later. If you have a telephone conversation with somebody, get a record of it so that you can go back later and recall exactly what was discussed. Sometimes it can take years for things to play out. Memories fade and opinions can differ over time. Having a written record is important because it memorializes discussions. Documentation is no silver bullet against disputes, but proper documentation can play a major role in resolving disputes.

The Goal of Passive Income

There are different models and ways people can generate money, and most of us as orthopaedic surgeons look at ourselves and think we are business owners, but we really are professionals—highly paid employees. We do not typically generate income unless we are working. We do not generally use Leverage.

Passive income—or income generated on a regular basis with little effort—is a key concept and is a goal for many. We are truly financially free when our passive income exceeds our monthly expenditures.

In the meantime, we use retirement and benefit plans, we invest in rental real estate, and we use some of the other tools mentioned in this book so that we can work towards financial freedom. Most of us want to get to that point where we have passive income so that our revenue/income is not entirely predicated upon how hard we work, how long we work, or how many surgeries we do.

I don't think most orthopaedic surgeons realize that. Many do not realize that there are ways to generate passive income. To realize your full economic potential, you have to do more than just work harder, work more hours, and perform more surgeries.

Wealth Protection

One point that is often overlooked in financial planning is that you don't need to hit a homerun to become wealthy in this game. Physicians are generally paid well, and as long as you save appropriately and make smart investments where you are not going to lose your principal, and get a reasonable return, then with compounding interest, you are going to eventually acquire a considerable nest egg in 20-30 years.

"Rule #1 is don't lose principal. Rule #2 is never forget Rule #1." This is solid advice that I agree with. Protect what you earn.

Of course, we are not taught how to invest in our medical training. We get no financial literacy courses. We are not taught about managing people. We are not taught about tax reduction strategies. We are not taught about the different types of business structures. So it is really important for orthopaedic surgeons to find the experts and develop relationships with the right financial team that will help educate us in these areas.

I have learned that there are many different types of investments. Some investments fit better from a wealth–protection mode than others. Wealth protection may mean a shield from taxes or simple asset protection.

I have learned how certain assets that I didn't know existed or didn't have any idea how they worked, work well in my particular financial situation. My co-authors have included information about some of these ideas in this book—like cash value life insurance, captive insurance companies, and qualified and non-qualified benefit plans, among others.

Even assets like our homes, which many of us used to believe always went up in value, might not be such a good investment,. The whole country learned in the last five years that home prices don't always go up! What we thought was an asset—our home—actually becomes a liability.

We all have colleagues who spend more than they should on depreciating assets—like cars or boats, etc. Always think twice before you jump into buying something that will be a depreciating asset. Think about the wisdom of Ben Franklin, who wrote about frugality as a virtue. Accumulating and protecting your wealth must be the foundation of your long-term financial plans.

It's What You Keep that Matters

Finally, focus on what you actually keep. When it comes to your income or your investments, you have to focus on what you get AFTER expenses, AFTER taxes, AFTER fees. Many of us are now working until August or September just to pay our practice overhead and taxes! With overhead generally running around 50% and taxes taking out 50% of what's left, we are only retaining about 25% of what we generate throughout the year—and that 25% has to pay our living expenses BEFORE we can invest for our future.

Consider your investments as well and be sure to understand the expenses involved (commissions, fees, etc.) and what type of taxes the investment will spin off. You will be unpleasantly surprised at how little of the investment gains actually end up in your pocket without pro-active planning.

Quarterback Role

One of the most important things I had to learn (sometimes the hard way) was that I was not an expert in every area. For most of us orthopaedic surgeons and sports medicine specialists, we have spent a lot of time training to do what we do. However, very few of us have much experience in other areas—especially areas concerning financial, tax, and legal issues.

Having a team of trusted advisors is crucial. In my opinion, you need a team to help you manage corporate structures, tax issues, asset protection, financial planning, insurance, and accounting.

How will you manage this team of advisors? How will you even know what questions to ask? How will you coordinate with them so that nothing falls through the cracks and make certain all the planning is top-notch?

The bottom line is this: As a practicing physician, you cannot do all this and manage all these areas on your own. We are not trained to do it, and we don't have the time, anyway. This is why I think it is so important to develop a relationship with an advisor who can fill the role of a quarterback, someone on the field who understands all the aspects and who understands what the other advisors are doing. You need someone who can speak with them on their level and can coordinate with them and act as your personal CFO.

I am glad that I found my co-authors, Jason and David. Their firm has been my financial quarterback over the last few years. They have worked with my other advisors, and as a result, my planning has improved greatly.

Investment Management: How to Build Wealth in Up, Down & Sideways Markets

From David Mandell, JD, MBA, Jason O'Dell, MS, CWM and Carole Foos, CPA

TRIAGE SUMMARY: If you want your assets to build wealth for your retirement, you need to find a firm that has a business model aligned with your goals. Also, over the long term, utilizing investment techniques that can build wealth in up, down, and sideways markets is crucial.

Choosing an Investment Firm

Five Important Questions May Give You The Answer

As financial advisors to hundreds of physicians throughout the U.S. and lecturers to thousands more, we have seen a sharp increase in the last few years in questions about how investment firms, including ours, make money from their clients. Physicians are not alone, as a 2011 survey by Cerulli Associates and Phoenix Marketing International found that nearly 2 out of every 3 investors in the survey were confused about how they were paying their advisors.[1]

This issue made headlines again in 2012, as a high ranking Goldman Sachs employee resigned publicly through an Op-Ed piece in the New York Times, citing corporate culture as the primary reason for his departure. The employee stated "the interests of the clients continue to be sidelined in the way the firm operates and thinks about making money." If this occurs at Goldman Sachs, whose clients include the most sophisticated financial firms in the world, it can certainly also occur at any physician's chosen investment firm.

In this section, we will attempt to educate you on five questions to ask your financial advisor in order to better understand how they make money from you and how they work for, or potentially against, you.

---

[1] Jerry Gleeson, "You Charge What?," WealthManagement.com (2012): Accessed August 28, 2012. http://wealthmanagement.com/practice-management/you-charge-what

Question #1: Does your advisor owe you a fiduciary duty as a client, or are they held only to a "suitability" standard?

Most physician investors are not aware of the fact that brokers and investment advisors are held to different standards when it comes to the duty they owe clients. Registered Investment Advisors such as OJM Group are held to a "fiduciary standard." This means that we are required to make recommendations that are in the client's best interest. Contrast this duty to the suitability requirement that dictates that brokers are simply required to make recommendations that are suitable based on the facts at the time of the interaction. On the surface, this may seem like a subtle difference; however, the end result can have a substantial impact on the client.

Example: Client A contacts his broker and expresses an interest in investing $50,000 in U.S. growth stocks. The broker invests the client assets in Fund XYZ, which charges a sales load of 5.75% with operating expenses of 0.68% annually. The client will immediately pay a one-time fee of $2875 on the trade on top of the recurring fund–management fee. In this case the suitability standard has been met. Client B contacts his Registered Investment Advisor with the same request. The investment advisor purchases an ETF with a gross expense ratio of 0.18% and pays a commission of $8.95 on the trade. This client pays his RIA a management fee of 1% of the assets, which equates to $500 per year on $50,000. The advisor has met the fiduciary standard. In our very realistic example, the front loaded fees paid by client A are significant enough that it would require a commitment of approximately nine years to this fund family before that commission is equal to the sum of advisory fees paid by client B.

Question #2: Can your advisor provide a detailed explanation of how they are compensated?

Do they receive commissions on any of the investments they will be recommending? Beyond commissions, compensation can come from sales charges on mutual funds or from a higher operating expense on a specific class of funds. A registered investment advisor such as OJM typically has access to an institutional class of funds which will charge a lower expense than the retail shares commonly offered by brokers. Private equities, structured notes, hedge funds, and non–traded REITs can offer various fees arrangements that may not be transparent. These investments may have a higher point of entry for an investor under the brokerage model in order to compensate the sales person facilitating the transaction. A Registered Investment Advisor operating under the fiduciary standard may be able to offer the same investment at a lower cost simply due to the fact that they are not taking a cut before your money goes to work for you.

Example: Client A is approached by his broker to invest in a non-publicly traded real estate investment trust. The client sends in a check for $100,000, and the security is priced at $10 per share, so the client receives 10,000 shares. The broker receives a 7% commission from the real estate investment trust sponsor. Client B is approached by his RIA to invest $100,000 in the same privately held REIT. The advisor charges a 1% management fee and does not accept compensation from the REIT sponsor. In this scenario, the commission is returned to the RIA client in the form of a reduced purchase price for the shares. Client B receives a discounted price of $9.30 from the sponsor and is able to purchase 10,752 shares of the same REIT with his $100,000 investment. Client A would have to hold the investment for approximately seven years before his 7% commission matches the sum of fees paid by client B to his advisor.

Question #3: Does your advisor's firm make money in other ways on your individual investments?
Request clarification on the ways that your advisor's firm may receive financial benefit from the securities you

own in your portfolio. As an example, mutual funds commonly offer revenue–sharing arrangements with a broker– dealer firm. In this scenario, your advisor at broker-dealer firm XYZ is receiving security analysis provided by its research department, which creates a buy list of securities. Unbeknownst to you, XYZ receives compensation from the fund company offering the recommended products. The result is a higher fee to you, the investor. You will not see these fees appear as a line item on your statement; they will be hidden within the underlying investments. This lack of transparency will not only prevent a client from recognizing the true cost of the relationship; it may also create a bias in the research provided to the client's advisor. This scenario can apply to closed end funds, exchange traded notes, and other securities which will impact the bottom line of the firm, even if your investment representative may not receive additional compensation.

Example: Discount brokerage firm XYZ offers to manage client assets at a reduced cost of 0.80% of assets under management for Client A. The rep at XYZ purchases $150,000 of retail shares of a bond fund with an operating expense of 0.75%. The rep does not receive compensation for choosing this fund; however, his firm (XYZ) receives revenue sharing directly from the fund company. A registered investment advisor for client B charges 1% for his services and purchases institutional shares of the same fund with an operating expense of 0.46%. RIAs often have access to the lower cost shares offered by certain mutual fund families. In this scenario, the discount brokerage relationship results in a slightly higher cost to client A because of hidden revenue sharing, despite the brokerage charging a lower management fee for their service.[2]

---

[2] Operating expenses represent actual net expense ratio as of 7/31/2012 of Pimco Total Return Fund Class D PTTDX and Pimco Total Return Fund Institutional Class PTTRX

Question #4: Does your advisor utilize proprietary securities?

Proprietary products are not always easily recognizable, as they can be branded under a different name. In-house products are not necessarily poor investments at the moment the recommendation is made to a client. The problem arises when circumstances change and it is no longer in a client's best interest to continue to own the underlying security. Will the in-house research recommend that their team of advisors liquidate the position in each of the firm's client accounts? Consider the impact of mass redemptions in a proprietary security. Who is going to be on the other side of that trade?

Example: XYZ firm runs a highly rated international bond fund with heavy exposure to European bonds. A team of brokers are looking out for their clients and contacts their research team to express concern about the recent drop in price of the investment. The research team of XYZ assures the brokers that they have adequately hedged the portfolio. A month later, concerned about the potential liability of a poorly performing investment, XYZ firm removes the fund from the institutional portfolios they are managing. The large redemptions create a significant drop in the price of the fund. A notification is then sent to the brokers explaining the firm's position after the price drop has occurred. The individual investor has faced substantial losses, while the firm has minimized the damage to their largest institutional clients.

Question #5: Does the advisor's firm engage in investment banking activities?

If the answer is yes, determine how your financial professional (and the firm) is compensated on your purchase of that investment. What is the incentive of the firm to see that the entire offering is filled?

Example: There are countless examples of Initial Public Offerings where individual investors have been sold on tales of tremendous growth opportunities, only to experience disappointing returns and a substantial loss on their investment. The recent handling of the high profile IPO of Facebook resulted in numerous lawsuits and continues to raise questions about the inherent conflicts in the underwriting process.

The Diagnosis

We recognize that this is not a complete list of the questions you should be asking your current or prospective advisor. One of our objectives in this section was to help you identify the potential conflicts in a traditional brokerage relationship, where costs are often much higher than they initially appear. A registered investment advisor such as OJM Group typically will charge a fee that represents a percentage of the assets managed and does not receive compensation from the investments that are recommended. Our hope is that by asking the questions we have listed above, investors will have a greater understanding of the potential factors that may influence the recommendations of their advisor. If every trade made on your behalf is not unequivocally for your benefit, it is time to reevaluate the relationship you have with your financial service provider.

4-2

How to Build Investment Wealth in Up, Down & Sideways Markets

---

Your Investments MUST Work for You Today

As a sports medicine physician, you know that building wealth is a challenge. Whether it is the federal government's unrelenting efforts to cut reimbursements, private payers following suit, increasing overhead, or recent tax increases (with more potentially on the horizon), it is truly harder for orthopaedic surgeons to build wealth today than in any time over the last 40 years.

The fact is that nearly all specialists and surgeons have to work harder than before to reach their financial goals. However, this hard work doesn't have to be performed by you alone. For successful orthopaedic surgeons seeking to meet their financial goals, it is critical that their assets shoulder some of the burden.

> The bottom line: If you want to meet your financial goals
> and retire on your own terms, your assets—
> most importantly, your investments—must work for you.

Unfortunately, most physicians do not have their investments working hard enough for them. Do you?

As Peter mentioned above, you don't have to hit a home run investing, but you do want to get a reasonable return over the long haul. In this chapter, you may learn some insights on how to do that. Here, we will provide a brief background on how securities markets have performed since the 1920s and discuss how you can build and sustain wealth by putting your investment dollars to work in up, down and *sideways* markets.

While you have likely seen and heard a lot about investments and the markets before, we are confident that you have not seen the data and approach to the markets that you will see here.

Background on U.S. Markets: Volatility, Trending Up

Most of you, as orthopaedic surgeons, review or have even taken part in scientific studies. The sample size is one of the most important factors in determining the validity of any study. The same holds true for investing. Physicians are trained to review data dispassionately. Still, too many physicians base important investment decisions on information from short samples—leading to emotional and irrational decisions.

Basing investment strategies on one–year, three–year or even five–year sample sizes can lead to long–term headaches. In our review, we will look at over 90 years of historic data from the Dow Jones Industrial Average (DOW), and 85 years worth of data from the Standard and Poor 500 Index (S&P). We will also go outside the boundaries of the U.S. stock market and review 40 years of data from the Japanese Nikkei 225. This means we will use 217 years of market data in our analysis. You may be accustomed to seeing larger studies in medicine, but we bet you haven't been presented many investment studies using this significant a sample size before.

The DOW and the S&P

Any extended view of the DOW or the S&P shows that, over the long–term, the securities market has varied greatly year to year. However, both markets have historically trended upwards. There are up periods and some down periods, and there are periods where the market has grinded along sideways while slowly inching higher. A steady investor can make money in the long run if they employ strategies that take advantage of upswings, diminish losses during down periods, and make steady gains during sideways markets.

You have probably seen charts illustrating the potential of growing your money in the stock market. It is worth looking at again. The following charts show how much $1 invested in the DOW in 1920 and $1 invested in the S&P in 1928[3] would be worth today.

---

[3] Prior to 1957, the S&P index was made up of 90 stocks. The S&P 500 in its present form began in 1947.

4.2.1 Present Value of $1 Invested in the DOW in 1920, Bloomberg, LP

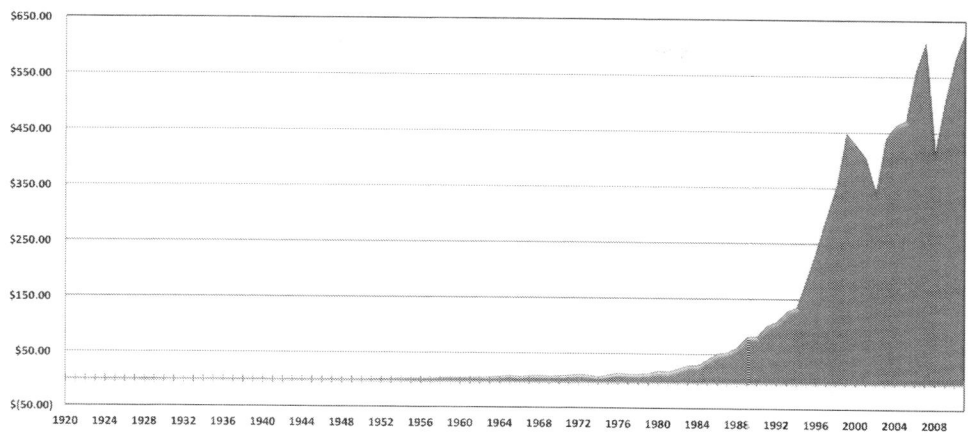

4.2.2 Present Value of $1 Invested in the S&P in 1928, Bloomberg, LP

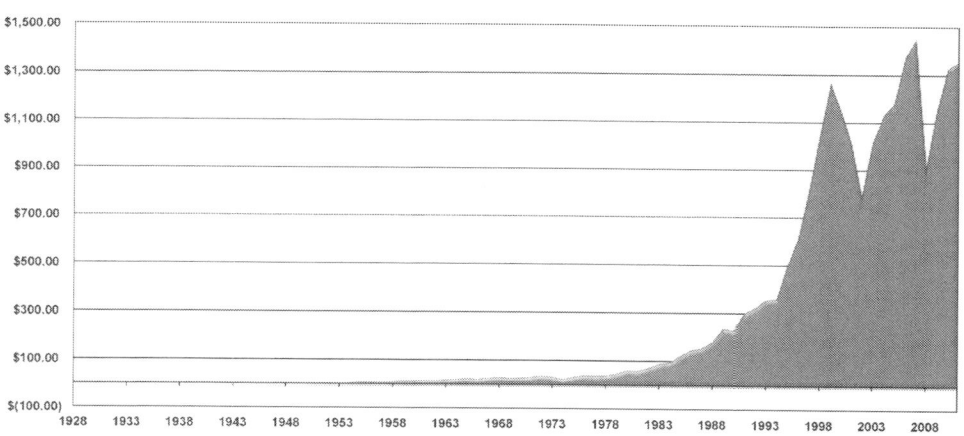

The reason these charts are worth a look is they are clear evidence of the historical long–term trend of both markets. Despite great year–to–year volatility, both markets have moved upwards over the long term over the last 80–90 years.

For further illustration, let's look at the raw numbers, the year–by–year actual returns of the DOW from 1920–2012 and the S&P from 1928–2012. These numbers are instructive because they demonstrate the actual year–to–year swings in both markets. Note how random the numbers are. Some periods can be tied to historical events: negative years around the Great Depression and positive years around the Dot.Com Boom. Yet there is no discernible pattern in the year–to–year fluctuations. Even if you could detect a pattern, it would make no difference in determining future projections.

4.2.3 Dow Jones Industrial Annual Returns: 1920-2012: Source: Bloomberg, LP

Year	Return	Year	Return	Year	Return
1920	32.9	1951	14.4	1981	(-3.6)
1921	12.3	1952	8.4	1982	27.1
1922	21.5	1953	(-3.8)	1983	26.0
1923	(-2.7)	1954	44.0	1984	1.3
1924	26.1	1955	20.8	1985	33.6
1925	30	1956	2.3	1986	27.1
1926	0.3	1957	(-12.7)	1987	5.5
1927	27.7	1958	34.0	1988	16.1
1928	49.5	1959	16.4	1989	32.2
1929	(-17.2)	1960	(-9.3)	1990	(-0.6)
1930	(-33.8)	1961	18.7	1991	24.1
1931	(-52.7)	1962	(-10.8)	1992	7.4
1932	(-22.6)	1963	20.8	1993	17.0
1933	63.7	1964	18.8	1994	5.0
1934	5.4	1965	14.4	1995	36.9
1935	38.5	1966	(-16.0)	1996	28.9
1936	24.8	1967	19.2	1997	24.9
1937	(-32.8)	1968	7.9	1998	18.1
1938	27.7	1969	(-11.8)	1999	27.2
1939	(-2.8)	1970	9.2	2000	(-4.7)
1940	(12.6)	1971	9.3	2001	(-5.4)
1941	(-15.4)	1972	18.5	2002	(-15)
1942	7.6	1973	(-13.3)	2003	28.3
1943	13.6	1974	(-23.6)	2004	5.3

Year	Return	Year	Return	Year	Return
1944	11.82	1975	44.8	2005	1.8
1945	26.9	1976	22.8	2006	19
1946	(-8.1)	1977	(-12.8)	2007	8.9
1947	2.2	1978	2.7	2008	(-31.9)
1948	(-2.1)	1979	10.5	2009	22.7
1949	13.1	1980	22.2	2010	14
1950	17.4			2011	8.4
				2012	8.84

4.2.4 S&P 500 Annual Returns 1928-2012
Source: Bloomberg, LP

Year	Return	Year	Return	Year	Return
1928	37.9	1957	(-10.7)	1986	18.7
1929	(-11.9)	1958	43.1	1987	5.3
1930	(-28.5)	1959	11.9	1988	16.6
1931	(-47.1)	1960	0.5	1989	31.7
1932	(-14.8)	1961	26.9	1990	(-3.1)
1933	44.1	1962	(-8.7)	1991	30.5
1934	(-4.7)	1963	22.7	1992	7.6
1935	41.4	1964	16.4	1993	10.1
1936	33.7	1965	12.4	1994	1.3
1937	(-34.7)	1966	(-10)	1995	37.6
1938	30.1	1967	23.9	1996	23
1939	(-0.1)	1968	11	1997	33.4
1940	(-9.6)	1969	(-8.4)	1998	28.6
1941	(-11.6)	1970	3.8	1999	21
1942	20.1	1971	14.3	2000	(-9.2)
1943	25.6	1972	19.2	2001	(-12)
1944	19.5	1973	(-14.3)	2002	(-22.1)
1945	36.3	1974	(-26.5)	2003	28.7
1946	(-8)	1975	37.2	2004	10.9
1947	5.6	1976	23.9	2005	4.9
1948	5.4	1977	(-7.2)	2006	15.8

Year	Return	Year	Return	Year	Return
1949	23.6	1978	6.6	2007	5.5
1950	32.6	1979	18.6	2008	(-37)
1951	23.8	1980	32.5	2009	26.5
1952	18.2	1981	(-4.9)	2010	15
1953	(-0.9)	1982	21.5	2011	2.1
1954	52.3	1983	22.6	2012	16
1955	31.4	1984	6.2		
1956	6.5	1985	31.7		

The charts above demonstrate the past annual volatility of the DOW and S&P. The long–term upward trend is not as apparent here, but the great year–to–year fluctuations in both markets should be clear. These charts are very important, and we will refer to them throughout this analysis.

A Note about Market Timing

Before we get too far along, we feel obligated to discuss investors who attempt to time the market. Market timing is as old as the markets themselves. Since the beginning, investors have attempted to take advantage of positive years and get out before the negative years. As the charts above demonstrated, there really is no rhyme or reason for discerning when the market will rise or fall. Predicting when markets will be positive or negative is virtually impossible.

A few pros on Wall Street may be able to have some success in this type of trading over the very short term (and they are often computers running quantitative analysis programming), but it is debatable if any individual human or computer has been successful doing this over the long run. If someone was truly able to time the market successfully over the long term, he or she would be the wealthiest person in the world. Warren Buffet, the professional investor with the world's greatest net worth, famously eschews market timing. He favors long–term investments in companies and industries he finds attractive.

Interestingly, it is quite clear from data that individual investors, unlike Mr. Buffet, get crushed when they try to time the market. This is because of the basic human emotions GREED and FEAR. In countless studies, retail investors have shown repeatedly that they will buy into the market near the top of a cycle—when their greed kicks in ("The market has been going up. I want in on this!")—only to sell at close to the market's low when fear rules the day ("The market is getting killed. I better get out before it's too late!")

Morningstar released a study[4] in 2010 that showed the devastating price investors pay in attempting to time the market. Morningstar monitored mutual fund investors' cash flow for ten years. They used investor returns to determine how the average investor fared during the decade. The total return for the average investor in all funds between 2000–2009 was 1.68%, compared with 3.18% for the average fund itself. Morningstar determined that most investors read too much into recent performance—letting fear and greed influence their decisions, making bad situations worse.

Investors lost over 47% of the fund performance due to their market timing decisions. In other words, an investor who did not try to time the market, but stayed in for the highs and lows, performed nearly 94% better than those who tried to time it.

Conclusion

Long–range views of the DOW or the S&P show that the securities market has varied greatly annually but has historically trended upwards. Investors can build wealth in the long run if they create a plan that accounts for periods of instability in the marketplace and avoid the pitfalls of market timing.

Now that we have a background on the two broad equity market returns for the last 90+ years, let's dig a bit deeper and understand what history can tell us about *up*, *down*, and *sideways* markets. For the remainder of this chapter, we will focus on the S&P. If you would like corresponding information on the DOW, please see our upcoming special report that you can download for free on our website: www.ojmgroup.com.

---

[4] Bad Timing Eats Away at Investor Returns; Russel Kinnel; February 15, 2010.

Up Markets

Up Markets Defined

It stands to reason that it should to be easy to maximize investments and accumulate wealth during an up market period—but how do you define an up market? Also, would you recognize an *up* market in time to take advantage of it?

If we define an up market as a five–year period during which the S&P continued to rise for five consecutive years, or at least four out of five years, you would find this occurred relatively frequently:

4.2.5 1928-2007: 52-out-of-81[5]
UP Periods in the S&P: Bloomberg, LP

1941-45 (4-1)	1959-63 (4-1)	1986-90 (4-1)
1942-46 (4-1)	1960-64 (4-1)	1987-91 (4-1)
1934-47 (4-1)	1961-65 (4-1)	1988-92 (4-1)
1944-48 (4-1)	1963-67 (4-1)	1989-93 (4-1)
1945-49 (4-1)	1964-68 (4-1)	1990-94 (4-1)
1946-50 (4-1)	1967-71 (4-1)	1991-95 (5-0)
1947-51 (5-0)	1968-72 (4-1)	1992-96 (5-0)
1948-52 (5-0)	1975-79 (4-1)	1993-97 (5-0)
1949-53 (4-1)	1976-80 (4-1)	1994-98 (5-0)
1950-54 (4-1)	1978-82 (4-1)	1995-99 (5-0)
1951-55 (4-1)	1979-83 (4-1)	1996-2000 (4-1)
1952-56 (4-1)	1980-84 (4-1)	2002-06 (4-1)
1954-58 (4-1)	1981-85 (4-1)	2003-07 (5-0)
1955-59 (4-1)	1982-86 (5-0)	2004-08 (4-1)
1956-60 (4-1)	1983-87 (5-0)	2005-09 (4-1)
1957-61 (4-1)	1984-88 (5-0)	2006-10 (4-1)
1958-62 (4-1)	1985-89 (5-0)	2007-11 (4-1)
		2008-12 (4-1)

---

[5] The last five-year period is 2008-12. The S&P has been up every year between 2009-2012

4.2.6 S&P 500 Index Annual Return: 1928–2011

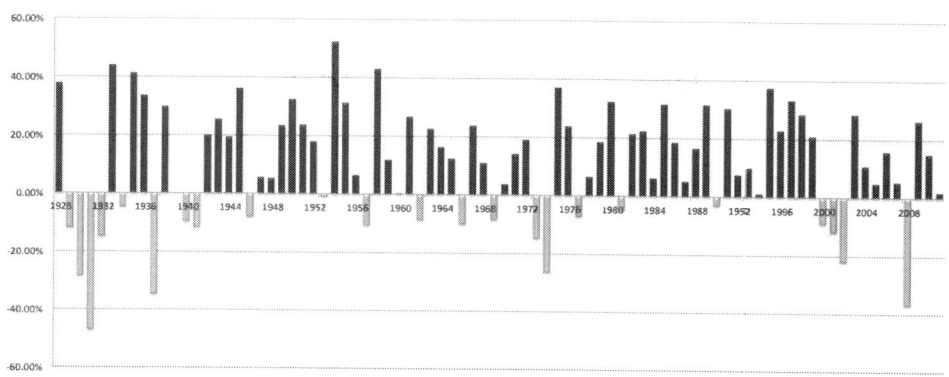

The preceding charts show that roughly 60% of the five–year periods have been *up* according to our definition. However, an *up* period does not guarantee an investor positive returns. It only takes one severe down year to wipe out four years of positive gains. Also, if you buy high during an up period, you could do further damage to your portfolio when the market levels.

Look at the S&P since 2000. In 13 years there have been nine years with positive returns and four years with negative returns. There was only one negative since 2003, but 2008 was so severe that the S&P was down nearly 40%. Many investors saw gains made during the nice run of positive years from 2003 through 2007 disappear in 2008. Thus, building wealth—even in up periods—can be tricky without a long–term investment strategy.

Boom Period (1982-1999): An Anomaly?

If you look at the above charts, you will see that the years 1982 through 1999 saw a historic run in the S&P—showing positive returns in 17 out of 18 years. The lone down year came in 1990.

Given the 85 years of S&P data, this long period of consistent positive returns is seemingly an anomaly. There are no other comparable periods, or anything even close to it. Part of the explanation might be simple supply–demand of securities. During this period, the entire Baby Boomer generation was in saving and investing mode. The youngest Boomers (those born in 1964), ages 18–35, were just beginning to save and invest. The oldest Boomers (those born in 1946), ages 36–53, were not yet in retirement liquidation mode. Certainly, other factors, such as the end of the Cold War, the Internet revolution, and interest rates and fiscal policy, played an important role in the period as well.

Regardless of the reasons, if we back out the anomalous years, the impact is notable. There were 61 positive years out of the 85 between 1928 through 2012—over 70%. If you take out the 18-year boom period, the percentage of positive years dips to 65%.

Now you know: Historically, there have been many up periods. How do you take advantage of these periods?

How to Build Wealth in Up Markets

If you suddenly found yourself in the middle of an *up* market, seemingly all you would need to do is blindly throw a dart at a list of stocks and watch the money roll in. It is not that easy. Despite consistent up periods, most investors' returns have been negative or flat for the past decade. This is often due to two factors:

1. Market timing: As discussed above, the problem is that many retail investors buy high and sell low.

2. Significant down years: 2002 and 2008 were two of the worst years in either index since the Great Depression. Without downside protection, gains made in positive years can be wiped out in market slides.

Given these challenges, how does one build wealth in up markets?

Diversification: The Golden Rule

The best and most time–tested method for protection of investment assets is diversification. Never forget that the root principle of diversification is the simple rule of not putting all your eggs in one basket.

Diversification is the Golden Rule of long–term investing—even during positive markets. Diversification through asset allocation among different types of investment options, and further diversification within these asset classes, is the hallmark of any successful portfolio. A truly diversified investment portfolio attempts to maintain the best possible expected level of return in relation to its level of acceptable risk. Modern Portfolio Theory is based on this simply described, yet complex to implement, concept.

Looking at the big picture and comparing six asset classes—large stocks, small stocks, long term government bonds, international stocks, treasury bills, and diversified portfolios—you will see that diversified portfolios were the most consistent performers, with all other classes showing great year–to–year volatility. The following chart shows different asset class winners from year to year, 1997–2012:

4.2.7 Asset Class Winners and Losers

	1998	1999	2000	2001	2002	2003	2004	2005	2006	2007	2008	2009	2010	2011	2012
HIGHEST RETURN	28.6	29.8	21.5	22.8	17.8	60.7	20.7	14.0	26.9	11.6	25.9	32.5	31.3	28.2	18.2
	20.3	27.3	5.9	3.8	1.6	39.2	18.4	7.8	16.2	9.9	1.6	28.1	15.1	3.1	17.9
	13.1	21.0	0.6	3.7	-6.5	28.7	12.0	7.3	15.8	5.5	-20.7	26.5	13.6	2.1	16.0
	12.2	14.3	-3.6	-0.8	-13.3	24.8	10.9	6.7	12.9	5.4	-36.7	14.0	10.1	0.0	11.3
	4.9	4.7	-9.1	-11.9	-15.7	1.4	8.5	4.9	4.8	4.7	-37.0	0.1	8.2	-3.3	3.3
LOWEST RETURN	-7.3	-9.0	-14.0	-21.2	-22.1	1.0	1.2	3.0	1.2	-5.2	-43.1	-14.9	0.1	-11.7	6.1

SMALL STOCKS   LARGE STOCKS   INTERNATIONAL STOCKS   LONG-TERM GOV'T BONDS

TREASURY BILLS   DIVERSIFIED PORTFOLIO

From 1997 through 2012:

1. Large stocks were winners twice and losers once.

2. Small stocks were winners four times and losers twice.

3. Long term government bonds were winners three times and losers three times.

4. International stocks were winners five times and losers five times.

5. Treasury bills finished second four times and last five times.

6. Diversified portfolios finished second once, and hovered in the middle of the pack every other year.

As the above chart demonstrates, yesterday's high–performing asset class can easily become tomorrow's loser. Even in positive markets, diversification is the golden rule—better performance with less risk.

No matter how diversified you are in the equities markets, if you are committing all your resources to the equities market, you are not truly diversified. While you may have hedged against some level of risk, you have not hedged against the risk of the entire market declining.

What We Learned about Diversification in 2008

Prior to 2008, proper diversification meant allocating among the major assets classes listed above—large cap, small cap, international, bonds, etc. However, this version of diversification was problematic because these major asset classes were strongly correlated. Many orthopaedic surgeons realized that this version of diversification was ineffective during major down swings that affected the entire equities market. Let's look at the asset classes' performance in 2008.

1. Large stocks: (–37.0)

2. Small stocks: (–36.7)

3. Long–term government bonds: 25.9

4. International stocks: (–43.1)

5. Treasury bills: 1.6

The other safe haven for stock market diversification many investors rely on is real estate. Yet property values fell equally hard in 2008. The S&P/Case–Shiller Home Price Indices (Case–Shiller) is the leading measure for the U.S. residential housing market. Case–Shiller reported its largest drop, 18.2%, in history in 2008. Thus, real estate as a stock market hedge simply did not work.

Other investors dabbled in hedge funds as a diversification tool, but they learned the hard way that many flash–in–the–pan hedge fund managers popularized with big gains in the early years of managing their fund rarely, if ever, maintain that momentum. Strong hedge fund performers attracted many investors in the late 1990s. Unfortunately, the majority of these funds took a beating in 2008. The average hedge fund performance that year was a loss of 23%[6] —not really much of a hedge.

Taxes: A Crucial Factor in Long-Term Investing

As Peter noted above, it's what you keep that matters. Although most of the investment community ignores it, tax consequences must be considered when weighing any investment decision. Your bank, fund manager, broker etc., is typically only concerned about pre–tax returns (figures on which their bonus is based and which they use in their marketing materials). You are concerned with the dollars in your pockets, not those that go to the IRS or state. The difference between pre–tax and post–tax figures can be significant.

According to mutual fund tracker Lipper, over the 20 years between 1987 and 2007, the average investor in a taxable stock mutual fund gave up the equivalent of 17-44% of their returns to taxes.[7] That is a lot of money and a broad range. When it comes to taxes, what you don't know can hurt you. Intelligent investors understand that an investment portfolio is not managed in a vacuum. Investment decisions must factor in tax consequences. Investors can employ tax-loss harvesting techniques to offset capital gains. Spreading investments out across different types of accounts can also work to lessen the burden. Finally, investing in tax-advantaged asset classes can help an investor accumulate wealth rather than see their returns gutted by taxes.

Conclusion

The data clearly shows that historically, the equities markets have trended up. However, despite such an up trend, poor market timing and significant (if less frequent) down years have made wealth accumulation elusive, especially in this last decade. Traditional stock market hedges like real estate or hedge funds haven't helped much, if at all. Further, even if you have managed to make some gains,

---

[6] Buttonwood, *Rich Managers, Poor Clients*, January 7, 2012, The Economist, access on March 26, 2013 at http://www.economist.ccm/node/21542452)

[7] http://www.ojmarticles.com/2012/05/dont-let-another-april-15th-be-rainy.html

Uncle Sam still gets his cut. All these factors make it difficult to accumulate wealth—even during the good times.

The solution is proper diversification in equities and other investments. You must try to limit your downside exposure and be tax–savvy. In order to build investment wealth over the long haul, you must remain disciplined.

Down Markets

As you have seen in the above charts, negative market years have thus far been relatively rare in comparison with positive years. Historically, there have been few periods of consecutive negative years in the U.S. markets.

Still, as you know by now, a single negative market year can wipe out gains accumulated over many consecutive positive periods. The objective in getting through these periods is to mitigate losses so they do not wipe out all the gains made during rising markets.

Down Market Periods Defined

If we define a *down* market the same way we defined up markets above—five consecutive years of negative returns, or four out of five years with negative returns—you will see that markets historically rarely go down for a long period without at least a few up years.

4.2.8. Down Periods for the S&P: Bloomberg, LP

1928-32 (1-4)	1929-33 (1-4)	1930-34 (1-4)	1937-41 (1-4)

Note: There has not been a single five–year period in the history of the S&P with five straight years of negative returns.

Most people with a passing knowledge of American history have heard the stories about the Great Depression. Would it surprise you to learn that between the years of 1929 and 1940, the S&P posted three years with positive returns? Markets still experienced positive years, even during the worst economic crisis in history.

What should also jump out from the information above is that long–term *down* markets have been rare in the U.S. That is not to say they may not happen more frequently in the future, but history demonstrates that the market *has rarely been down for more than two straight years*:

4.2.9 Years of Consecutive Down Periods in the S&P: Bloomberg, LP

1929-1932	4 years
1939-1941	3 years
1973-1974	2 years
2000-2002	3 years

Going Forward

Despite the data above, many investors now believe that the U.S. market is moving in a different direction. Many factors, such as globalization, the U.S. debt, the poor economy, and gridlock in Washington, D.C., weigh on investors and provide for gloomier outlooks. We should not just look to our past to understand how markets may work in the future. The U.S. might look more like other countries that have experienced long–term steep declines in their stock markets.

In order to examine the possibility of a long–term decline in the U.S. securities market, we will examine the most prominent stock market decline of a major global industrialized nation: the decline of Japan's Nikkei 225 stock market since the early 1990s.

Case Study: The Nikkei

The Nikkei is the broad stock market for the Japanese economy, similar to the DOW. Many powerhouse companies are listed on the Nikkei, including Sony, Toyota, Honda, and Mitsubishi. The Nikkei had a tremendous 20–year run from 1970 through 1990. It was volatile during this time frame, but it was mostly upward volatility, as the next chart clearly shows:

4.2.10. NIKKEI from 1970 through 2011: Bloomberg, LP

Value of a $10,000 Investment in the Nikkei in 1971

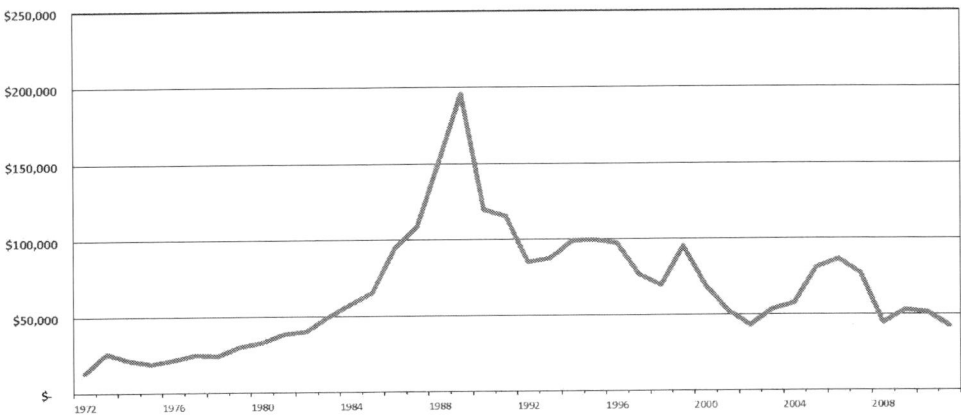

However, as you can see, starting in 1990 and continuing through today, the Nikkei lost more than 60% of its value. The index peaked in December of 1989 at 38,916, and by December of 2011, it had declined to 8,458. As we discussed, markets in the U.S. have not experienced any similar long–term market declines, but as the Nikkei shows, it's possible.

Note: During this precipitous decline, there were still no *down* periods of five out of five, or even four out of five down years during a single five–year period. Also, consider how many positive years there were, even in the Nikkei's historic down market. Even though it decreased by 60% in value from 1990–2011, there were still many positive years mixed in as the market slid. In fact, nearly half of the years were positive—nine out of those 20 years! See next chart:

4.2.11. NIKKEI Returns 1991-2010.
Source: Bloomberg, LP

Value of a $10,000 Investment in the Nikkei in 1990

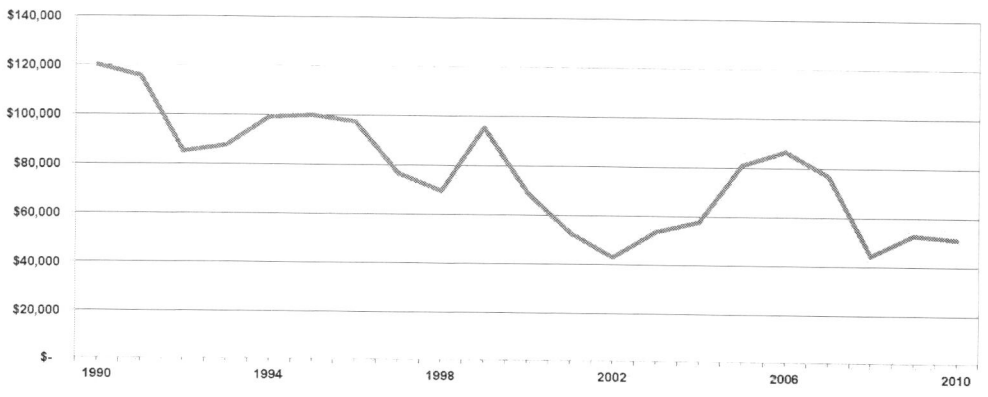

4.2.12

1991	(-3.63)	9,637
1992	(-26.36)	7,097
1993	2.91	7,303
1994	13.24	8,270
1995	0.74	8,331
1996	(-2.55)	8,118
1997	(-21.19)	6,398
1998	(-9.28)	5,804
1999	36.79	7,939
2000	(-27.19)	5,780
2001	(-23.52)	4,421
2002	(-18.63)	3,597
2003	24.45	4,477
2004	7.61	4,817
2005	40.24	6,756
2006	6.92	7,223
2007	(-11.13)	6,419
2008	(-42.12)	3,715
2009	19.04	4,422
2010	(-3.01)	4,289

Not only were there nine positive years, but many of the years were up significantly. There were huge positive years where surely some investors in the Nikkei were able to take advantage of the market. In fact, there was even an *up* market within our definition above during this down trend, four straight positive years (2003–2006) in the middle of one of the most historic down trends in one of the world's largest stock markets.

Even if we assume that the U.S. markets could be in for a multi–year negative decline that they have not experienced before, if Japan is a model for such a decline, then we could expect the period to include many positive years.

Making Money in Short-Term Down Markets

Obviously, it is difficult to make money when the markets are showing negative returns. If individual stocks, asset classes, and markets are all declining, how do investors make money?

Shorting is one trading technique investors have used for de-cades to take advantage of down markets. When an investor goes *short* on a security, they are anticipating a decrease in the share price. The investor borrows funds from a third–party broker with the intent of buying the security back at a later date. The investor is attempting to sell something high *now*, and buy it back at a lower price *later*. The investor is betting against the security and profiting from the anticipated decline in price of the security.

The short seller will incur a loss if the price of the security rises, since the investor will have to buy the securities back at a higher price than they sold them. There are also other costs of shorting, including fees for borrowing the assets and payment of any divi-dends paid on the borrowed assets. By definition, *shorting* is not a long–term investment strategy. Shorting is a trading technique sometimes attempted to make a gain when a security or market is trending down over the short term. Shorting is essentially another way to try to time the market.

It is extremely difficult to build wealth in down market peri-ods without taking on larger risk. Techniques like shorting may generate gains, but they are risky and not considered long–term investment strategies. The key to long–term successful investing is to not lose too much in down periods.

Conclusion

Historically, there have not been long–term declines in the U.S. markets since the 1920s. Even in the Nikkei's severe down trend, there were many significant upswings dotting the landscape. Wise investors do not panic in down markets, and some have found ways to take advantage of upticks by following long–term investment strategies.

Sideways Markets

We have looked at *up* markets and *down* markets, and how historically up markets have been far more common than down markets. What about the common *sideways* market? How do you accumulate and sustain wealth when the market is flat?

Sideways Markets Defined

We specifically define a *sideways* market as a five–year period wherein there are at least two years with positive returns and at least two years with negative returns. These are important market periods to understand because they have occurred relatively frequently.

Many investment advisors discuss *ad nauseam* the gains they made during positive markets and how they beat the market during negative market periods. However, these same advisors usually ignore the frequent sideways markets. The best long–term investment strategies should attempt to account for all market conditions.

For the last 80–plus years, the U.S. stock market has inched along with periods of growth followed by years of decline—wash, rinse, repeat. See the S&P:

4.2.13 S&P, 25-out-of 81 periods were Sideways: Bloomberg, LP

1931-35 (2-3)	1953-57 (3-2)	1974-78 (3-2)
1932-36 (3-2)	1962-66 (3-2)	1977-81 (3-2)
1933-37 (3-2)	1965-69 (3-2)	1997-2001 (3-2)
1934-38 (3-2)	1966-70 (3-2)	1998-02 (2-3)
1935-39 (3-2)	1969-73 (3-2)	1999-03 (2-3)
1936-40 (2-3)	1970-74 (3-2)	2000-04 (2-3)
1938-42 (3-2)	1971-75 (3-2)	2001-05 (3-2)
1939-43 (2-3)	1972-76 (3-2)	
1940-44 (3-2)	1973-77 (3-2)	

Over 30% of the five–year periods in the S&P were sideways. If you take out the 1982–1999 anomaly period, then sideways periods jump to 38% of the S&P.

Given this significant percentage of time, it makes sense that if you cannot make gains during *sideways* markets, you simply cannot build wealth.

What Does this Mean For Investing?

Let's take a hypothetical 11–year time period wherein every year it switches up, then down by the same incremental amount: year one up 10%, year two down 10%, year three up, year four down, and so on. You would assume that at the very least you would break even. However, as you will see, if you do nothing to mitigate the losses taken in the down years, you will not gain and you will not break even. You will actually lose money over time.

The assumption of the average investor is that if the market is up as often as it is down and if all the swings are equal, then we should at least break even. That assumption is incorrect, and we will show you why, starting with $1,000:

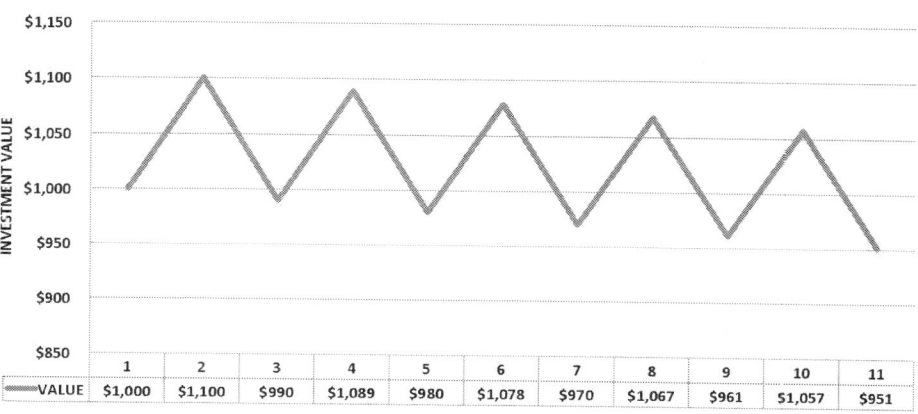

4.2.14 Value of $1,000 invested gaining and losing 10% per year for 10 years

VALUE	1	2	3	4	5	6	7	8	9	10	11
	$1,000	$1,100	$990	$1,089	$980	$1,078	$970	$1,067	$961	$1,057	$951

Have you spotted the trend? The $1,000 you started with would eventually turn into $951. Your average rate of return would be zero, but your actual rate of return would be –4.9%.

Even if you were lucky enough to pull your investment during a positive year, your initial investment did little to grow. Rather, it bounced back and forth—up one year, down the next. And, of course, this hypothetical market did not include expenses, like investment manager fees or taxes. So how does an investor make money in a *sideways* market?

Making Money in Sideways Markets: Introduction to "Floor and Cap" Indexing

An investment product investors have employed to handle market unpredictability is "floor–and–cap" indexing—generally done through cash–value life insurance products. This product also helps mediate tax consequences. The floor–and–cap principle works by employing a set floor for losses and a set ceiling for gains tied to a specific market index, like the DOW or S&P.

We will discuss a floor of 0% and cap of 13% here, but there is a wide range of caps and floors out in the marketplace.

A 0–13% floor–and–cap follows a market index. When the market has a year with negative returns, the product fixes a floor of 0% return. If the product is tied to the S&P, and that year realizes negative returns of 10%, indexing will fix the investor's return to zero. Rather than seeing any loss, the investment will remain flat. Let's apply indexing to a couple of different examples:

4.2.15 Indexing of the $1,000 investment

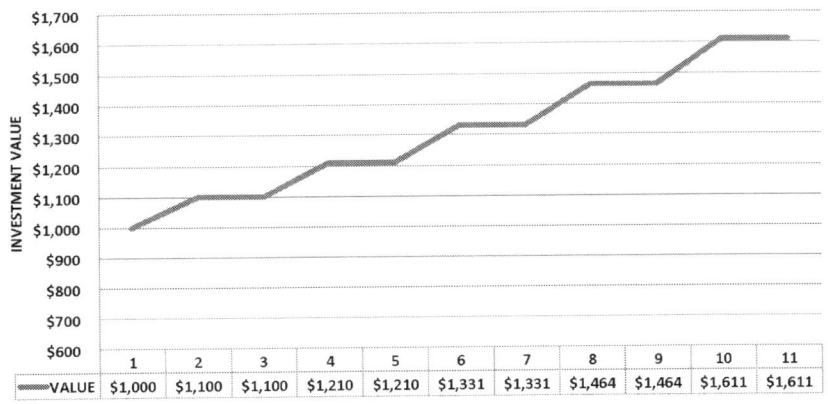

VALUE	1	2	3	4	5	6	7	8	9	10	11
	$1,000	$1,100	$1,100	$1,210	$1,210	$1,331	$1,331	$1,464	$1,464	$1,611	$1,611

Chart 4.2.14., above, showed the $1,000 investment jumping up and down, year to year. Chart 4.2.15. shows how indexing the investment minimizes losses to zero in any one year, thus providing for a steady upward trend. It seems too good to be true, so let's review use of indexing in another example, the S&P.

4.2.16. Cap and Floor Indexing versus S&P. Bloomberg, LP

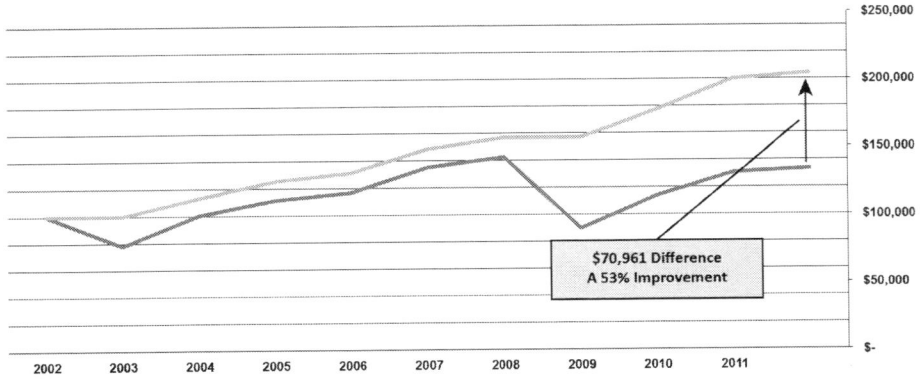

$70,961 Difference
A 53% Improvement

Value of $100,000 Invested in the S&P 500 Index, excluding dividends, in 2002 *(Lower Line)*

Value of $100,000 Using the Floor and Cap Indexing Strategy *(Upper Line)*

Chart 4.2.16 demonstrates how utilizing a 0–13% floor and cap may be used to build wealth in today's equity markets. As you can see, a floor/cap strategy would have significantly out–performed a standard investment in the S&P over the last 10 years. Note that they tracked evenly until 2008, when the straight S&P investment suffered a massive decline. With a floor–and–cap investment product, the growth was steadier since there were no declines in value. In 2008, the floor–and–cap investment was still worth $156,700. Also, as the market came back in 2009–2012, most of the gains were captured by the strategy as well.

Overall, the difference between the two strategies is significant. Many physicians see this chart and can relate to the blue line: Their assets have not helped them grow wealth much over the last decade.

Now, let's see what happens when we employ the indexing strategy with the historical Nikkei—since many bearish investors worry that such a decline is what the U.S. markets may be facing in the future. If the capped/floored product turned every negative year into a 0% rate of return, and then captured every positive year up to a maximum of 13%, here's what it would look like:

4.2.17 Nikkei versus "Floor and Cap"—Bloomberg, LP

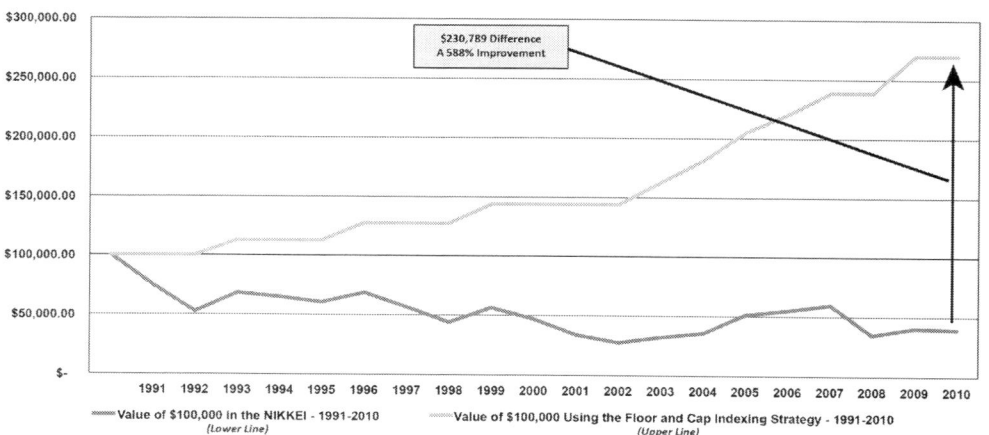

$230,789 Difference
A 588% Improvement

Value of $100,000 in the NIKKEI - 1991-2010
(Lower Line)

Value of $100,000 Using the Floor and Cap Indexing Strategy - 1991-2010
(Upper Line)

4.2.18. Nikkei 225 Index: Annual Returns

Using indexing strategy (13% cap)

	Year	Beginning Year Value	Gain/Loss % for Year	Gain % Credited	Gain/Loss for Year	Year End Value
1	1991	$1,000,000	-25.50%		$0	$1,000,000
2	1992	$1,000,000	-29.40%		$0	$1,000,000
3	1993	$1,000,000	29.70%	13.00%	$130,000	$1,130,000
4	1994	$1,130,000	-4.80%		$0	$1,130,000
5	1995	$1,130,000	-7.00%		$0	$1,130,000
6	1996	$1,130,000	13.70%	13.00%	$146,900	$1,276,900
7	1997	$1,276,900	-17.60%		$0	$1,276,900
8	1998	$1,276,900	-22.30%		$0	$1,276,900
9	1999	$1,276,900	28.70%	13.00%	$165,997	$1,442,897
10	2000	$1,442,897	-17.10%		$0	$1,442,897
11	2001	$1,442,897	-28.20%		$0	$1,442,897
12	2002	$1,442,897	-18.70%		$0	$1,442,897
13	2003	$1,442,897	16.80%	13.00%	$187,577	$1,630,474
14	2004	$1,630,474	11.40%	11.40%	$185,874	$1,816,348
15	2005	$1,816,348	43.80%	13.00%	$236,125	$2,052,473
16	2006	$2,052,473	7.50%	7.50%	$153,935	$2,206,408
17	2007	$2,206,408	8.30%	8.30%	$183,132	$2,389,540
18	2008	$2,389,540	-42.20%		$0	$2,389,540
19	2009	$2,389,540	17.30%	13.00%	$310,640	$2,700,180
20	2010	$2,700,180	-3.00%		$0	$2,700,180
			270.0% increase in value from 1991			
			Denotes a Positive Year			

As the charts above demonstrate, by removing all the negative years and capping positive returns at 13%, you have an increase in value of over 270% instead of a loss of more than 60%. That is a difference in this case of over $2.3 million on a $1 million initial investment.

How Can an Investor Utilize "Cap & Floor" Indexing?

The *indexing* strategy can be employed via **a cash value equity–indexed universal life (IUL) insurance policy**. That is a lot of jargon, so let's break it down:

For starters, what we are alluding to here is a *life insurance policy*: a contract between a policyholder and an insurer, where in exchange for payment from the policyholder (premium), the insurer promises to pay a beneficiary, designated by the insured, a sum of money (benefit) upon the death of the insured person.

Cash value is the value of the policy contract itself—i.e., the policyholder may make withdrawals of past premiums paid and take out loans against the total value of the death benefit.

A *universal life insurance policy* combines permanent life insurance coverage and flexibility in premium payments (both lump sums and regular payments) with the potential for growth of cash values by means of permitting the premiums and cash value to function as an investment tool.

Note: When considering the spectrum of risk associated with different investment tools, products, or strategies, an IUL is on a par with a bond, as the insurance company's assets back up its guarantees, just as a corporate bond issuer backs up its bond payments. An IUL, however, is a complex tool that is heavily customized to the policyholder. It is not a one–size–fits–all investment option.

A unique feature of an indexed universal life policy is that it offers protection from negative returns from a negative market period. The protection is provided by way of a minimum guaranteed interest rate, or "floor" rate, usually between 0–2%. There will also be a corresponding "cap", or maximum amount of interest credited to the policy during positive markets, generally ranging between 10–15%. The movement of value of the policy is dictated by an index like the S&P.

As we discussed above, the S&P returns are extremely variable (see Chart 4.2.5). The average (mean) return in the S&P since 1928 is 11.06%. That said, you cannot expect 11% annual returns regardless of your investment strategy. The S&P rises and falls at differing rates every year. As you know, the S&P experienced 24 years of negative returns since 1928. For these 24 years, the average (mean) negative return was −14.42%; with −37% recently, in 2008.

Obviously, the S&P has traditionally experienced many more years with positive gains. In fact, if you take the 61 positive years, the average (mean) return is 21.08%. By reviewing the average low, the average high, and the overall average, you see a wide range of possibilities for the S&P on a year–to–year basis.

You cannot time or predict the swings in the S&P. You can, however, use a conservative Cap and Floor IUL to hedge against some of your more aggressive investments to close the gaps between the peaks and valleys of the market.

By removing all the negative years and capping positive returns at 13%, you have an increase in value of over 270%, rather than a loss of more than 60%. That is a difference in this case of over $2.3 million on a $1 million initial investment.

How Can an Investor Utilize "Cap & Floor" Indexing?

Let's examine how floor–and–cap indexing inside a universal life policy (IUL) compares with a more common equity fund investment.

Comparison: Cap & Floor IUL vs. Brokerage Account

To demonstrate the utility of floor and cap indexing, we will compare a scenario with a 45–year–old male who invests $100,000 a year for five years, for a total of $500,000. The investor then makes no further contributions and takes no additional action involving the investment until reaching the age of 65.

We will assume that once the investor reaches 65, they will start withdrawing a stream of income from the 25–year savings for annual retirement income.

Based on the data above, we know that on average the market experiences three years with negative returns during each ten–year period. For our comparison scenario, we will include a few additional assumptions:

- Federal Income tax rate of 39.6%, a state income tax rate of 5%, and additional tax (payroll, local, etc) of 3.8%

- 20% of the investment gains will be taxed as short–term income and the remaining 80% taxed at the long–term capital gains rate

We will further assume a 7% average rate of return for both investments. However, in every third year, we will assume a negative 7%. Therefore, the typical investment will experience a loss of 7% three times a decade—but the IUL will simply have a 0% rate of return for these negative years. While one could certainly suggest alternative assumptions—and we encourage you to contact us so we can run different scenarios for you—we do think these represent a conservative approach.

How will the two investments compare?

The investor who put their $500,000 in the market starting at age 45 will be able to withdraw $40,121 per year starting at age 65 for 14 years, through age 78. The investor will have a remaining balance of $34,831 for the final year. The total value of the investment is $596,524.

Note: During the course of the investment, the investor will pay approximately $212,567 in taxes.

Using all the same assumptions, we will now see what happens if the investor puts $100,000 per year for five years starting at the age of 45, into an IUL (total investment of $500,000). At the age of 65, the investor will be able to withdraw $65,001 per year for 15 years. The total value of the investment is $975,015. The potential power of the IUL's superior tax treatment, combined with the cap and floor strategy, out–performed the typical brokerage account investment by $378,491—an improvement of more than 63%!

For a year–by–year breakdown of how each option compares, please see the charts on the next page.

4.2.19. Brokerage Account Holder, 45 year-old, $500,000 Investment

Year	Age	Investment	Begin Balance	Net Annual Investment	Gross Investment	Gross Investment Gain (7%)	Taxes	Ending Balance	Withdrawal
1	45	$100,000		$100,000	$100,000	$7,000	$2,290	$104,710	$0
2	46	$100,000	$104,710	$100,000	$204,710	$14,330	$4,689	$214,351	$0
3	47	$100,000	$214,351	$100,000	$314,351	($22,005)	$0	$292,346	$0
4	48	$100,000	$292,346	$100,000	$392,346	$27,464	$8,986	$410,824	$0
5	49	$100,000	$410,824	$100,000	$510,824	$35,758	$11,700	$534,882	$0
6	50	$0	$534,882	$0	$534,882	($37,442)	$0	$497,440	$0
7	51	$0	$497,440	$0	$497,440	$34,821	$11,393	$520,867	$0
8	52	$0	$520,867	$0	$520,867	$36,461	$11,930	$545,398	$0
9	53	$0	$545,398	$0	$545,398	($38,178)	$0	$507,220	$0
10	54	$0	$507,220	$0	$507,220	$35,505	$11,617	$531,108	$0
11	55	$0	$531,108	$0	$531,108	$37,178	$12,165	$556,122	$0
12	56	$0	$556,122	$0	$556,122	($38,929)	$0	$517,193	$0
13	57	$0	$517,193	$0	$517,193	$36,204	$11,846	$541,551	$0
14	58	$0	$541,551	$0	$541,551	$37,909	$12,404	$567,056	$0
15	59	$0	$567,056	$0	$567,056	($39,694)	$0	$527,362	$0
16	60	$0	$527,362	$0	$527,362	$36,915	$12,079	$552,198	$0
17	61	$0	$552,198	$0	$552,198	$38,654	$12,648	$578,205	$0
18	62	$0	$578,205	$0	$578,205	($40,474)	$0	$537,730	$0
19	63	$0	$537,730	$0	$537,730	$37,641	$12,316	$563,055	$0
20	64	$0	$563,055	$0	$563,055	$39,414	$12,896	$589,573	$0
21	65	$0	$589,573	$0	$589,573	($41,270)	$0	$508,182	$40,121
22	66	$0	$508,182	$0	$508,182	$35,573	$11,638	$491,994	$40,121
23	67	$0	$491,994	$0	$491,994	$34,440	$11,269	$475,044	$40,121
24	68	$0	$475,044	$0	$475,044	($33,253)	$0	$401,670	$40,121
25	69	$0	$401,670	$0	$401,670	$28,117	$9,200	$380,466	$40,121
26	70	$0	$380,466	$0	$380,466	$26,633	$8,714	$358,264	$40,121
27	71	$0	$358,264	$0	$358,264	($25,078)	$0	$293,064	$40,121
28	72	$0	$293,064	$0	$293,064	$20,514	$6,712	$266,745	$40,121
29	73	$0	$266,745	$0	$266,745	$18,672	$6,110	$239,187	$40,121
30	74	$0	$239,187	$0	$239,187	($18,743)	$0	$182,323	$40,121
31	75	$0	$182,323	$0	$182,323	$12,763	$4,176	$150,788	$40,121
32	76	$0	$150,788	$0	$150,788	$10,555	$3,454	$117,789	$40,121
33	77	$0	$117,789	$0	$117,789	($8,244)	$0	$69,404	$40,121
34	78	$0	$69,404	$0	$69,404	$4,858	$1,590	$32,552	$40,121
35	79	$0	$32,552	$0	$32,552	$2,279	$746	$0	$34,831
				$500,000			$212,567		$596,524

4.2.20. Scenario: IUL Policyholder, 45-years old, $500,000 Investment

Insurance Premium	Withdrawal	Net Accumulated Value	Net Cash Surrender Value	Death Benefit	Improvement Over Brokerage Account
$100,000	0	71,071	31,170	2,173,633	$0
$100,000	0	150,659	130,708	2,253,221	$0
$100,000	0	223,222	205,266	2,325,784	$0
$100,000	0	319,750	303,789	2,422,312	$0
$100,000	0	425,773	411,808	2,528,335	$0
$0	0	410,764	398,794	2,528,335	$0
$0	0	425,483	415,508	2,528,335	$0
$0	0	444,688	436,709	1,051,304	$0
$0	0	435,953	431,962	1,051,304	$0
$0	0	457,511	457,511	1,051,304	$0
$0	0	492,240	492,240	1,051,304	$0
$0	0	491,447	491,447	1,051,304	$0
$0	0	528,518	528,518	1,051,304	$0
$0	0	568,354	568,354	1,051,304	$0
$0	0	567,172	567,172	1,051,304	$0
$0	0	609,572	609,572	1,051,304	$0
$0	0	655,178	655,178	1,051,304	$0
$0	0	653,579	653,579	1,051,304	$0
$0	0	702,307	702,307	1,051,304	$0
$0	0	754,819	754,819	1,051,304	$0
$0	65,001	688,026	688,026	986,303	$24,880
$0	65,001	671,451	671,451	921,302	$24,880
$0	65,001	653,670	653,670	856,301	$24,880
$0	65,001	586,816	586,816	791,300	$24,880
$0	65,001	562,325	562,325	726,299	$24,880
$0	65,001	532,242	532,242	661,298	$24,880
$0	65,001	465,538	465,538	610,608	$24,880
$0	65,001	428,088	428,088	590,510	$24,880
$0	65,001	387,987	387,987	524,265	$24,880
$0	65,001	320,682	320,682	456,529	$24,880
$0	65,001	273,061	273,061	387,269	$24,880
$0	65,001	222,315	222,315	316,451	$24,880
$0	65,001	155,239	155,239	244,039	$24,880
$0	65,001	96,427	96,427	169,998	$24,880
$0	65,001	33,737	33,737	94,291	$30,170
	$975,015				$378,491

Many factors could alter the above results. We present the above as a simple example to show how cap and floor indexing compares to investing in securities. It is important to note that the IUL policy design is key in extracting the kind of performance illustrated above.

The results above are not guaranteed. Furthermore, these comparisons are not typical *for out of the box* IUL policies with standard level death benefits. Rather, these policies are heavily customized predicated on the investor's intentions and circumstances. Without the right design, the IUL could underperform the straight market investment during a *sideways* market period.

As with any investment, you and your advisor must determine what is right for you. If you determine that an IUL is the right choice, you must also choose the right IUL policy. Then you must tailor the policy specifically to your planning objectives, and further manage the policy to maximize retirement income while complying with the numerous IRS rules. As is the case with any sophisticated financial approach, expert guidance is a necessity.

When Does IUL Cap & Floor Make Sense?

An IUL is not for everyone. This product is for investors focused on the long run with an eye towards retirement and steady accumulation of wealth. The IUL can be designed to minimize tax consequences and provide some life insurance benefits. This is not a liquid product. It should not be used for maximizing short–term gains. If you are not sure whether this product is right for you, talk to an expert.

Cap and Floor Summary

Historically, *sideways* market periods are common and generally a difficult environment for the retail investors, like physicians, to build wealth. Cap and floor indexing can be a strong option for part of a portfolio to take advantage of the *up* market periods while providing downside protection—especially for long–term investors looking to generate retirement income. As with any complex financial technique, proper professional guidance is crucial.

The Diagnosis

Everyone is working harder today—especially physicians. Many investors have lowered their expectations based on the market conditions of the last few years. It is important to assess and reassess financial goals from time to time, but you should not lose sight of the end goal. Building and sustaining wealth is not impossible. It's just tougher than it used to be.

The fact is that we cannot predict on any given day if the market will decline. We cannot know how low a market will go in any given time period. That said, we do know that there will be periods with negative returns in the market. The key is to be prepared and to get your assets to work for you.

In order for orthopaedic surgeons to get their money to truly work for them and build wealth, they must work with an advisory firm with the right incentives and proper focus on taxation issues. Most importantly, the client has to trust the advisor. The relationship must be transparent. Just as a patient must trust their doctor while following a long–term course of treatment, the doctor must trust their investment advisor while engaging in a long–term investment strategy.

Spend 25 Minutes to Build $250,000 in Additional Retirement Wealth

With Peter and Cheyenne, we created this short book because we know that you are extremely busy.

The same is true for many orthopaedic surgeons when it comes to a high level of planning: Even though it may save them taxes, build them wealth for retirement, and protect what they've worked so hard to acquire, they never get to it.

That is why we want our process to be efficient with your time. If we can get on the phone for just 25 minutes, we can determine if we can help you with your leading wealth planning concerns—whether that is a comprehensive plan, a review of your asset protection planning, tax reduction, corporate structure, insurances, or investments. And, yes, we will be able to determine if one or more of the tools we have used for hundreds of physicians across the county might work for you—to save tens of thousands of dollars per year in taxes and/or create hundreds of thousands of dollars of additional retirement wealth for you.

Our consults are always complimentary, and we can speak with you during the workday, in the evening, or on the weekends. Please give us a call at 877.656.4362 or email us at mandell@ojmgroup.com or odell@ojmgroup.com.

David B. Mandell
JD, MBA

Jason M. O'Dell
MS, CWM

Carole C. Foos
CPA

FREE CONSULTATION

Find out if you qualify for our "Firm Commitment."

OJM's Firm Commitment is a promise to qualifying clients that, if we can't suggest improvements that save you twice as much as the consulting fee you pay us, we will refund our fee in full. With this promise, we only earn our fee if we can provide truly quantifiable value to your practice.

We have helped over 1,000 physicians like you

- Reduce their income taxes by $5,000-$200,000 annually

- Shield their practice and personal assets from lawsuits

- Implement a more tax–efficient corporate structure

- Utilize superior qualified, non-qualified, and fringe benefit plans

- Build their investable wealth in a conservative, tax-savvy manner

- Coordinate all areas of planning

- And more.

**Please visit www.ojmgroup.com
or call (877) 656-4362
to schedule your FREE consultation.**

For Doctors Only: A Guide to Working & Building More teaches doctors the important lessons they never learned in medical school, residency or fellowship. Doctors learn how to efficiently leverage their time, money and effort so they can get more out of a medical practice. More specifically, doctors learn how to protect their personal and practice assets from lawsuits, taxes and bad investments while showing them the secrets to building wealth and avoiding catastrophic financial disasters. For Doctors Only is a MUST HAVE for any physician wishing to achieve financial success. Get a copy now!

For New York Doctors: A Guide to Asset Protection, Tax Reduction, Practice & Wealth Management teaches doctors the important lessons they never learned in medical school, residency or fellowship. Doctors will learn how to efficiently leverage their time, money and effort so they can get more out of a medical practice. More specifically, doctors learn how to protect their personal and practice assets from lawsuits, state-specific taxes and bad investments in addition to learning the secrets to building wealth and avoiding catastrophic financial disasters so they get the most out of their practice and leave the most for their heirs. *For New York Doctors* is a MUST HAVE for any New York doctor wishing to achieve financial success.

For Georgia Doctors: Fresh Ideas on Asset Protection, Practice Planning, Wealth Accumulation and Estate Planning teaches doctors how to handle the unique challenges of practicing medicine in Georgia so they will get more out of their medical practice and personal finances. Reduced reimbursements, higher taxes, and significant liability risk make it imperative that Georgia doctors work "on their practice" not just "in their practice" if they want to achieve any reasonable level of financial security. *For Georgia Doctors* is a MUST HAVE for any Georgia doctor wishing to achieve financial success.

For Ohio Doctors: Shedding Light on Asset Protection, Tax and Estate Planning teaches doctors how to handle the unique challenges of practicing medicine in Ohio so they will get more out of their medical practice and personal finances. Reduced reimbursements, higher taxes, and significant liability risk make it imperative that Ohio doctors work "on their practice" not just "in their practice" if they want to achieve any reasonable level of financial security. *For Ohio Doctors* is a MUST HAVE for any Ohio doctor wishing to achieve financial success.

For California Doctors: A Guide to Asset Protection, Tax and Estate Planning teaches doctors how to efficiently practice so they can get more out of a medical practice. More specifically, *For California Doctors* will help doctors protect their personal and practice assets from lawsuits, taxes and bad investments while showing them the secrets to building wealth through the leverage of people, assets and effort. *For California Doctors* is a MUST HAVE for any California doctor wishing to achieve financial success. Get a copy now!

Risk Management for the Practicing Physician is nationally accredited for 5.5hours of Category I continuing medical education (CME) credits in risk management. Co-written by a practicing physician, an attorney and a financial advisor, this monograph includes chapters on: providing care in today's malpractice environment, liability and the doctor-patient relationship, managing diagnosis-related liability, minimizing risks of miscommunication, managing high risk communication areas, managing the dangers of drug therapy, non- medical liability risks for the practicing physician, and liability in the new health care system.

Get a Copy Now!

SCHEDULE A CME SEMINAR

Guardian Publishing's education experts have delivered seminars on asset protection, tax and estate planning that range from one to four hours for over 200 medical groups, associations, hospitals and organizations.

Guardian can provide the Category I CME enduring material <u>Risk Management for the Practicing Physician</u> to attendees, to provide a CME component. In some instances, seminars can be created to generate revenue for an association. In other situations, seminars can be arranged for only the costs of travel and materials.

Please contact Guardian Publishing at 513-792-1252 to discuss the logistics of arranging this important seminar for you.

www.guardpub.com

REQUEST AUTHORS' ARTICLES
FOR YOUR PUBLICATION

The authors of Guardian Publishing have written eight books
for physicians and have written articles for over 100 periodicals,
newsletters and websites. The authors have also appeared on
hundreds of radio shows and on Bloomberg and Fox television.

Guardian can provide the content to educational publications at no
cost, provided the articles include by-lines that instruct readers how
to reach the authors if they have questions or require some consulting
assistance.

If you are interested in publishing articles by the authors on asset
protection, practice management, retirement, insurance, tax and
estate planning, please contact Guardian Publishing at 513-792-1252.

www.guardpub.com

Made in the USA
Columbia, SC
19 September 2018